Student Activity Guide

Fashion!

by
Mary Wolfe
St. Michaels, Maryland

Publisher
The Goodheart-Willcox Company, Inc.
Tinley Park, Illinois

Introduction

This activity guide is designed for use with the text Fashion! Doing the activities will help you review and recall fashion concepts and facts presented in the text.

The activities in this guide are divided into chapters that correspond to chapters in the text. Read the text first and then try to complete the activities without looking back at the text. You should have the information needed to complete each activity. When you have completed an activity, refer back to the text to check your answers and complete any questions you could not answer.

This guide contains a variety of types of activities. Some of them, such as crossword puzzles and word mazes, have the "right" answers. These activities can be used to help you review for tests and quizzes. Other activities ask for opinions, evaluations, and conclusions that cannot be judged as "right" or "wrong." These activities are designed to encourage you to consider alternatives, evaluate situations thoughtfully, and apply information in the text.

The activities in this guide have been designed to be both informative and fun to do. This activity guide will help you apply fashion knowledge to your life, whether you choose to have a career in fashion or to just be an informed consumer.

Copyright 2002

By

The Goodheart-Willcox Company, Inc.

Previous editions copyright 1998, 1993

International Standard Book Number 1-56637-832-X

2 3 4 5 6 7 8 9 10   02   06 05 04 03

Contents

		Activity Guide	Text

Part One
Clothes and fashion

1 The Why of Clothes 7 11
   A. Clothing for Protection
   B. The Significance of Uniforms
   C. Reverse Thinking
   D. Past, Present, and Future
   E. The Mirror of Fashion
   F. Conformity and Individuality
   G. Clothing for Adornment

2 Knowing About Fashion 17 22
   A. Fashion Cycles
   B. Defining Terms
   C. Questionable Thoughts
   D. Fashion News
   E. Draped, Tailored, and Composite Clothing

3 Garment Styles and Parts 23 35
   A. Categorizing Styles
   B. Garment Terms Crossword
   C. Learning from Looking at Illustrations
   D. Combining Garment Parts into Total Designs

Part Two
Apparel Industries

4 The Development of Fashion 31 54
   A. Your Fashion Interest Rating
   B. Famous Fashion Designers
   C. Characteristic Work of Designers
   D. Extending Your Knowledge of Designers
   E. Fashionable Opinions
   F. A Fashion Interview

5 The Textile Industry and Home Sewing Patterns 39 67
   A. The Production of Fabrics
   B. Textile and Pattern Term Tree
   C. The Versatility of Textiles
   D. The Importance of Color
   E. Put Your Knowledge to the Test

		Activity Guide	Text

6 Apparel Production 47 80
    A. Tell the Difference
    B. Working as a Designer and a Stylist
    C. Personal Reactions
    D. Apparel Production Terms
    E. Analyzing Fashion Designs

7 Fashion Promotion and Selling 57 102
    A. Fill in the Blanks
    B. Noticing the Private Labels
    C. Differences Described
    D. Statements of Interest
    E. Retail Outlets
    F. From Beginning to End

Part Three
Textiles: The "Science" of Apparel

8 Textile Fibers and Yarns 65 120
    A. Fiber Facts
    B. A Spool of Fibers
    C. Chapter Content Clues
    D. Generic Names and Trademarks
    E. Fiber Uses

9 Fabric Construction and Finishes 73 147
    A. Practice with Fabric Construction
    B. Fabric Construction Terms
    C. Fabric Coloring and Printing Crossword
    D. Fabric Knowledge
    E. Fabric Finishes Scramble
    F. Identifying Fabrics

Part Four
Design: The "Art" of Apparel

10 The Element of Color 81 172
    A. Working with Color Schemes
    B. Color Fill-In
    C. Using Color for Effect
    D. Flattering Personal Coloring

11 More Elements of Design 87 191
    A. Shape
    B. Creating with Lines
    C. Texture
    D. Line Categories and Illusions
    E. Analyze with Pictures

12 Principles of Design 95 205
    A. Unscramble the Terms
    B. Misfits and More Fits
    C. Analyzing "the Latest"
    D. Choose Flattering Outfits
    E. A Personal Style Analysis

Activity Guide	Text

Part Five
Consumers of Clothing

13 **The Best Clothes for You** 103 226
A. Reactions to Statements
B. Pictures and Words
C. A Personal Approach to Apparel
D. The Vocabulary Pyramid
E. Mixing and Matching

14 **Wardrobe Planning** 111 238
A. Write the Right Terms
B. The Final Analysis
C. Personal Reactions
D. Accessory Show and Tell
E. Record Your Resources

15 **Being a Smart Shopper** 119 254
A. Rating Retailers
B. Preparing Ahead
C. Laws that Relate to Consumers
D. Consumer Complaints
E. Smart Shopper Crossword
F. Shopping Manners

16 **Making the Right Purchase** 129 271
A. Ring Around the Letter
B. Comparison Shopping
C. Assemble the Words
D. Smart Consumer Maze
E. Purchasing Habits

17 **Apparel for People with Special Needs** 139 289
A. Special Needs Match-Up
B. Note the Similarities
C. A Special Needs Apparel Interview
D. Test Questions to Ask
E. Express Your Thoughts

18 **Caring for Clothes** 145 307
A. My Care of Clothes
B. Note the Differences
C. Laundry Product Comparisons
D. Storage Ideas
E. Laundering Selection
F. Follow the Label

		Activity Guide	Text

Part Six
Apparel Industry Careers

19 Careers in the Textile Industry 157 332
    A. Categorizing Jobs
    B. Textiles Careers
    C. Seeking Answers
    D. A Closer Look
    E. Read and React

20 Careers in Apparel Design and Production 165 349
    A. Job Titles and Descriptions
    B. You as a Designer
    C. Seeking Answers
    D. Qualifications for Careers
    E. Doing Market Research

21 Fashion Merchandising and Other Retail Industry Careers . . . 173 367
    A. Select an Occupation
    B. A Diamond of Retail Occupations
    C. The Retail Ladder Game
    D. Thoughts on Retail Employment

22 Careers in Fashion Promotion 179 384
    A. Career Categorizing
    B. Free-Lance Employment
    C. Fashion Journalism
    D. Truths and Falsehoods
    E. Add the Words

23 Other Careers and Entrepreneurial Opportunities 185 398
    A. Unscramble and Use
    B. Read and React
    C. Find Your Entrepreneurial Aptitude
    D. Planning Your Own Business
    E. Categorizing Occupations
    F. Follow Your Interests

24 A Career for You 195 418
    A. Definition Match-Up
    B. Differentiate
    C. Read and Think About It
    D. Employment Interests and Preparation
    E. Applying for Employment

The Why of Clothes

Clothing for Protection

Activity A   Name _____

Chapter 1   Date _____ Period_____

A. On the lines at the left, write the four main protective reasons that humans have worn clothing throughout history. On the lines at the right, list three articles of clothing that offer protection in each category.

1. _____   A. _____
   _____   B. _____
                                         C. _____

2. _____   A. _____
   _____   B. _____
                                         C. _____

3. _____   A. _____
   _____   B. _____
                                         C. _____

4. _____   A. _____
   _____   B. _____
                                         C. _____

B. Briefly write about an experience of yours that fits with one of the protective reasons for wearing clothing.

_____

_____

_____

_____

The Significance of Uniforms

Name _____

Date _____ Period_____

List five jobs or activities for which uniforms are worn. Then describe how each uniform looks. Finally, explain what meaning, feeling, or special importance is conveyed by the uniform.

Job or Activity	Uniform Description	Meaning, Feeling, or Special Importance
1. _____	_____	_____
_____	_____	_____
_____	_____	_____
2. _____	_____	_____
_____	_____	_____
_____	_____	_____
3. _____	_____	_____
_____	_____	_____
_____	_____	_____
4. _____	_____	_____
_____	_____	_____
_____	_____	_____
5. _____	_____	_____
_____	_____	_____
_____	_____	_____

Can you think of any reasons students or others might not prefer to wear uniforms?

_____

_____

_____

Reverse Thinking

Name _____

Date _____ Period_____

Write a question for each of the following answers based on the content of the chapter. Then, in a small group, read your questions to others and have them give you the correct answer without looking at the answer options.

1. For protection, adornment, identification, modesty, and status. _____

    _____

    _____

2. Physical need. _____

    _____

    _____

3. Psychological needs. _____

    _____

    _____

4. Social needs._____

    _____

    _____

    _____

5. Protective clothing. _____

    _____

    _____

    _____

6. Water-repellent garments. _____

    _____

    _____

    _____

7. Occupational clothing. _____

    _____

    _____

    _____

8. Bulletproof vests. _____

    _____

    _____

    _____

(Continued)

Name _____

9. Beauty. _____

_____

_____

_____

10. The fact that lots of money is spent each year on jewelry and beauty aids._____

_____

_____

_____

11. Uniforms. _____

_____

_____

_____

12. Rules of dress. _____

_____

13. A wedding gown._____

_____

_____

14. Dress codes. _____

_____

_____

15. A gown with decorative beading. _____

_____

_____

16. A fashion magazine from today should be left behind for people in the future. _____

_____

_____

_____

17. They are learned concepts from cultural customs and traditions; and economic and social conditions.

_____

_____

_____

18. These people are probably confident, outgoing, and secure. _____

_____

_____

Past, Present, and Future

Name _____

Date _____ Period_____

Read each statement about clothes that people wore in the past. Then write a related statement about clothes people wear today. Finally, predict four types of clothing that might evolve to meet the needs of people in the future. (Consider possible advances in technology; changes in attitudes about adornment, modesty, or status; and differences in careers and environmental controls.)

Past	Present
1. Fur pelts were worn around the body for warmth.	1. _____
2. Body shields and suits of armor protected the body from enemies.	2. _____
3. Decorations of animal bones, horns, teeth, shells, seeds, or feathers made the body more beautiful.	3. _____
4. All members of a specific tribe wore something particular on their skin or body to identify themselves with their group.	4. _____
5. A loincloth was worn below the waist even though the weather was warm enough to go without clothes.	5. _____
6. Hunters wore the pelts of their prey to show others how many and what kinds of animals they had killed.	6. _____

(Continued)

Future

7. _____
   _____
   _____
   _____
   _____

8. _____
   _____
   _____
   _____
   _____

9. _____
   _____
   _____
   _____
   _____

10. _____
   _____
   _____
   _____
   _____

The Mirror of Fashion

Activity E

Chapter 1

Name _____

Date _____ Period_____

1. If "fashion is a mirror of our times," explain what you think people 100 years from now might think about our culture after looking at today's fashion magazines. (Remember that 100 years ago, sunbonnets, parasols, top hats, floor-length skirts, and plain fabrics were common.)

_____

_____

_____

_____

2. Cut out current pictures of clothing that are examples of our times and mount them in the following three boxes. Write a short description of what the clothing in each picture might indicate.

A. _____

_____

_____

_____

_____

_____

_____

_____

_____

_____

_____

_____

_____

_____

_____

_____

_____

_____

_____

(Continued)

B. _____

_____

_____

_____

_____

_____

_____

_____

_____

_____

_____

_____

_____

_____

_____

_____

_____

_____

C. _____

_____

_____

_____

_____

_____

_____

_____

_____

_____

_____

_____

_____

_____

_____

_____

_____

_____

Conformity and Individuality

Activity F

Chapter 1

Name _____

Date _____ Period_____

1. Define *conformity.* _____

    _____

    _____

    _____

    _____

2. Describe two examples of clothing conformity among people in your school or community. _____

    _____

    _____

    _____

    _____

    _____

    _____

    _____

    _____

3. Define *individuality.* _____

    _____

    _____

    _____

4. Describe two examples of individuality expressed through clothing by people in your school or community.

    _____

    _____

    _____

    _____

    _____

    _____

5. Without naming the person, write down your thoughts about someone's personality as expressed by the way he or she dresses. _____

    _____

    _____

    _____

Clothing for Adornment

Name _____

Date _____ Period_____

Clip two pictures from magazines or catalogs that show clothes and accessories being used for adornment. Mount them in the following boxes. Then explain how each picture illustrates decoration being used to enhance attractiveness or beauty.

1. _____

_____

_____

2. _____

_____

_____

Fashion Cycles

Activity A

Chapter 2

Name _____

Date _____Period_____

1. Describe the stages of a typical fashion cycle. _____

_____

_____

_____

_____

_____

_____

_____

_____

_____

2. List five current apparel items and explain where you think each is in its fashion cycling process.

A. _____

_____

_____

B. _____

_____

_____

C. _____

_____

_____

_____

D. _____

_____

_____

_____

E. _____

_____

_____

Defining Terms

Name _____

Date _____ Period_____

Match the following terms and definitions by placing the correct letter next to each number.

_____ 1. Short, tapered stitched areas that enable a garment to fit the figure.

_____ 2. The selling of merchandise directly to consumers.

_____ 3. A recurring style with extra fullness at the back only.

_____ 4. A designer who creates original, individually-designed high fashions and usually owns the fashion house.

_____ 5. The selling of goods in large lots to retailers.

_____ 6. A particular design, shape, or type of apparel item.

_____ 7. The apparel area above the waist, usually closely fitted.

_____ 8. Articles of merchandise with slight imperfections that are sold to consumers at reduced prices.

_____ 9. All the garments and accessories a person owns.

_____ 10. Daring, wild, and unconventional designs.

_____ 11. Market categories based on retail selling prices of merchandise.

_____ 12. Garments made by a combination of the tailored and draped methods.

_____ 13. Trend-setting people who have enough status and credibility to introduce and popularize new styles.

_____ 14. A recurring style with fullness at the bottom.

_____ 15. The newest, most unique, and expensive apparel of fine quality and beautiful fabric, with limited acceptance.

_____ 16. Apparel items that are wrapped or hung on the body and have characteristic folds of soft fabric.

_____ 17. A style that is slim and straight from top to bottom.

_____ 18. Apparel made for the person who has ordered it, usually after seeing a sample garment, sketch, or picture.

_____ 19. Extra first-quality items produced by a manufacturer but not ordered by retailers.

_____ 20. Apparel items made by cutting garment pieces and then sewing them together to fit the shape of the body.

_____ 21. A garment or garment part that is shaped to follow the lines of the body.

_____ 22. Clothing that stays popular though fashions change.

_____ 23. Copies of other, usually higher-priced, garments.

_____ 24. Items that are soiled or have noticeable flaws and must therefore be priced lower than perfect goods.

_____ 25. The stealing of design ideas, or the use of a design, without the consent of the originator.

_____ 26. Apparel created specifically for a particular person with special fit, design, and fabric.

A. avant-garde clothes

B. back fullness silhouette

C. bell silhouette

D. bodice

E. classic

F. composite garments

G. couturier

H. custom-designed

I. custom-made

J. darts

K. draped garments

L. fashion leaders

M. fashion piracy

N. fitted

O. high fashion

P. irregulars

Q. knock-offs

R. overruns

S. price markets

T. retailing

U. seconds

V. style

W. tailored garments

X. tubular silhouette

Y. wardrobe

Z. wholesaling

Questionable Thoughts

Activity C

Chapter 2

Name _____

Date _____ Period _____

Write thought-provoking multiple choice questions for each of the following chapter sections. Write the letter of the correct answer for each question on a different piece of paper. Then exchange papers with class members to take one another's tests.

Fashion Terms:

1. _____

    A. _____

    B. _____

    C. _____

    D. _____

2. _____

    A. _____

    B. _____

    C. _____

    D. _____

Clothing Construction Terms:

3. _____

    A. _____

    B. _____

    C. _____

    D. _____

Clothing Business Terms:

4. _____

    A. _____

    B. _____

    C. _____

    D. _____

5. _____

    A. _____

    B. _____

    C. _____

    D. _____

(Continued)

Fashion Cycles:

6. _____

    A. _____

    B. _____

    C. _____

    D. _____

Social and Economic Influences on Fashion:

7. _____

    A. _____

    B. _____

    C. _____

    D. _____

Fashion News

Activity D

Chapter 2

Name _____

Date _____ Period_____

Find a current newspaper or magazine article that discusses a new fashion trend or spotlights one or more fashion leaders. Write your reactions to or comments about the article. Then cut out or photocopy the article and attach it to this page using a paper clip or staple.

_____

_____

_____

_____

_____

_____

_____

_____

_____

_____

_____

_____

_____

_____

_____

_____

_____

_____

_____

_____

_____

_____

_____

_____

_____

_____

_____

_____

_____

_____

_____

_____

_____

_____

_____

_____

_____

Draped, Tailored, and Composite Clothing

Name _____

Date _____Period_____

Either draw or cut out and mount pictures of draped, tailored, and composite clothes in the boxes. Then describe why the clothes fit into the different categories.

1. A draped garment:

This is a draped garment because _____

_____

_____

_____

_____

_____

_____

_____

_____

_____

_____

_____

_____

_____

_____

_____

_____

_____

_____

_____

_____

_____

_____

_____

(Continued)

2. A tailored garment:

3. A composite garment:

This is a tailored garment because _____

_____

_____

_____

_____

_____

_____

_____

_____

_____

_____

_____

_____

_____

_____

This is a composite garment because _____

_____

_____

_____

_____

_____

_____

_____

_____

_____

_____

_____

_____

_____

_____

Garment Styles and Parts

Categorizing Styles

Activity A

Chapter 3

Name _____

Date _____Period_____

Place four words from the following list in each of the general categories below. Use all of the words one time.

knickers	shift	saddle	horseshoe
bolero	windbreaker	jeans	gored
boat	bishop	pea	leg-o'-mutton
jumper	hip-huggers	chelsea	décolleté
dolman	trench	shirtwaist	coachman
wrap	coatdress	culottes	safari
jewel	button-down	puff	mandarin
raglan	dirndl	middy	French
umbrella	polo	petal	chesterfield

1. Dress styles:

_____

2. Neckline styles:

_____

3. Collar styles:

_____

4. Set-in sleeve styles:

_____

5. Other sleeve styles:

_____

6. Skirt styles:

_____

7. Pants styles:

_____

8. Coat styles:

_____

9. Jacket styles:

_____

Garment Terms Crossword

Name _____

Date _____ Period_____

Complete the crossword puzzle using the clues listed:

(Continued)

Across:

1. A sleeve style with a shaped seam in the garment originating from the underarm.
3. _____ skirts or pants become wider near the bottom.
7. A neckline that is draped with flowing folds.
8. A sweater that opens down the front.
9. Another name for a boat neckline.
11. A garment design with no sleeves.
12. A broad scarf worn at the neck like a necktie.
14. A dress style that has a high waistline.
15. Legs of pants that are narrower at the hem than at the knee are _____.
18. A kimono style sleeve that is very low and loose at the underarm.
20. A band at the bottom of a sleeve or pant leg.
23. A heavy winter jacket with a hood.
24. _____ are also called slacks or trousers.
25. A garment that slips over the head when put on or taken off.
27. A(n) _____ garment is shaped to follow the lines of the body.
29. A head covering that is attached at the neckline of a garment.
30. A hip-length or longer shirt that extends down over pants or a skirt and is sometimes belted.
33. A sleeve style that has a horizontal seam going around the upper part of the arm. (2 words)
36. A band of fabric that fastens together at the waistline of pants or skirts.
37. A long, flowing, robe-like garment.
38. A sleeveless, close-fitting, jacket-like garment that covers the chest and back.
39. A dress with a long torso is a waistline style.
41. A skirt with a slim silhouette and no added fullness.
42. Pants that are flared from the waistline and very full at the bottom.
44. Flared pants that are gathered in at the ankles.
45. A skirt that is gathered only slightly.
47. A closing that has a diagonal overlap to one side.
48. A dress style with blousy fullness in the top, usually with a fitted skirt and a belt.
49. A garment with a bottom (pants) attached to a top (bodice).
50. A band or shaped piece, usually at the shoulders or hips, to give shape and support to the garment below it.

Down:

2. A skirt style that has panels formed by vertical seamlines.
3. Decorative fabric pieces that fall down over the openings of pockets.
4. Long, loose garments worn over nightwear when not in bed.
5. Pants that end just below the knee with legs like wide tubes.
6. A cloak that hangs from the neck and shoulders and has no sleeves.
8. A collar style that can be worn closed at the neck or open to form a "V" shape with a lapel.
10. An opening that goes up into a sleeve from the cuff.
11. A dress that hangs from the shoulders and has inward shaping at the waist, but no waistline seam.
13. A ruffled or lace trimming effect on the front of men's or women's shirts going down from the neckline.
16. A built-in "envelope" in a garment to hold items.
17. A very short sleeve, sometimes called a French sleeve.
19. The fullness in _____ skirts is created by fabric being pulled together at the waist without structured folds.
21. A(n) _____ skirt has pleats or gathers.
22. A very full skirt that forms a circle when it lies flat.
24. A dress style with seamlines going up and down the entire length and no horizontal waistline seam.
26. A neckline that is lowered and round in front.
28. A wedge-shaped piece of fabric added to give more ease of movement at a kimono sleeve underarm or other area of a garment.
30. A decorative fabric piece that goes out from the edge of a pocket or other area of a garment.
31. A warm or weatherproof garment that is worn over regular clothing.
32. A classic jacket or sport coat.
34. Structured folds of cloth that give fullness in a garment.
35. A brief garment that is worn on the upper body.
39. Most suit jackets have _____ folded back at the front with the collar.
40. Another name for a shift dress.
43. _____ sleeves are continuous extensions out from the garment.
46. This large, billowy dress hangs loosely from the

Learning from Looking at Illustrations

Name _____

Date _____Period_____

shoulders.

Fill in the following blanks with the correct terms. Then write illustration numbers from the text that show examples of the terms.

1. A dress or skirt style that is narrow at the top and wider at the hemline is called _____.

   (#_____, #_____)

2. In a(n) _____garment, the right side is different from the left side. (#_____)

3. A dress for hot weather with a skirt attached to a brief bodice is called a(n) _____. (#_____)

4. A(n)_____, or jewel, neckline is plain and encircles the base of the neck.

   (#_____)

5. A(n) _____ collar is an imitation of an ascot. (#_____)

6. The decorative strip of fabric over the vent of a sleeve above the cuff is called a(n) _____.

   (#_____)

7. The seam on the inside of a pants leg, from crotch to hem, is called the _____.

   (#_____)

8. _____ jackets are held shut with one row of buttons. (#_____)

9. _____jackets have a wider overlap and two rows of buttons. (#_____)

10. A(n) _____ is an unshaped, blanket-like outer garment with a slit or hole in the mid-dle, so it can be slipped over the head. (#_____)

11. _____ dresses, a particular raglan sleeve design, and gored skirts have seamlines going ver-tically through the garment. (#_____, #_____, #_____)

12. _____ neckline and sleeve designs have draped, flowing folds. (#_____, #_____)

13. _____ collar and sleeve designs are most common for men's business attire. (#_____,

    #_____)

14. _____ sleeves have no seamlines connecting them to the garment bodice. (#_____)

15. The length of a(n) _____ skirt falls between the upper calf and midi lengths.

    (#_____)

Combining Garment Parts into Total Designs

Name _____

Date _____ Period _____

On each of these two figures, draw a particular outfit that shows your choice of a specific style of neckline, collar, sleeve, dress, skirt, or pants. You may also want to add options such as yokes, pockets, cuffs, tabs, and flaps. Name the styles of the parts of your total design next to each drawing.

1. _____

_____

_____

_____

_____

_____

_____

_____

_____

_____

_____

_____

_____

_____

_____

_____

_____

_____

_____

_____

2. _____
_____
_____
_____
_____
_____
_____
_____
_____
_____
_____
_____
_____
_____
_____
_____
_____
_____
_____
_____
_____

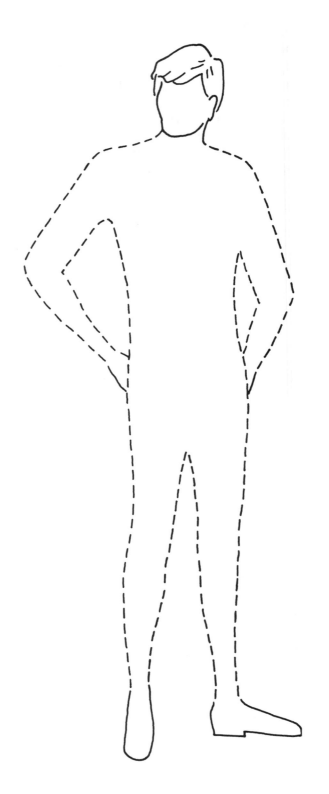

Chapter 4 | The Development of Fashion

Your Fashion Interest Rating

Activity A

Chapter 4

Name _____

Date _____ Period _____

In the blanks provided, check Always, Sometimes, or Never for each of the following statements. Tabulate your fashion interest rating by following the directions below. (You will not be graded on your rating!) Then complete the statement at the bottom of the page.

Statement	Always	Sometimes	Never
I read the newspaper fashion features and fashion magazines regularly.	_____	_____	_____
When I watch a movie or TV show, I notice what the actors wear.	_____	_____	_____
I enjoy looking through clothing catalogs.	_____	_____	_____
I recognize pictures of fashion designers.	_____	_____	_____
I can name the design firm of a garment by seeing the logo.	_____	_____	_____
I notice what my fellow students wear.	_____	_____	_____
I think about my apparel.	_____	_____	_____
I enjoy shopping for clothes.	_____	_____	_____
A fashion career interests me compared to other fields.	_____	_____	_____
When studying other countries and cultures, I find it interesting to learn about their apparel and fashions.	_____	_____	_____
When I see fashion news on TV, I think about becoming a famous fashion personality.	_____	_____	_____

To tabulate your rating, give yourself 4 points for each *Always* checked, 2 points for each *Sometimes* checked, and 0 points for each *Never* checked.
Your fashion interest rating: _____

If your total score is 35 or above, your fashion interest is high. If your score is 21 to 34, you have an average interest in fashion. A score of 20 or below means that fashion is probably not a big deal in your life!

I am surprised or not surprised about my fashion interest rating because _____

_____

_____

Famous Fashion Designers

Activity B

Chapter 4

Name _____

Date _____ Period_____

Using the charts and information in the text, write the last name of the correct fashion designer by each number according to the descriptions that follow:

1.							F				
2.							A				
3.							M				
4.							O				
5.							U				
6.							S				
7.							F				
8.							A				
9.							S				
10.							H				
11.							I				
12.							O				
13.							N				
14.							D				
15.							E				
16.							S				
17.							I				
18.							G				
19.							N				
20.							E				
21.							R				
22.							S				

1. This German native, based in France, designs for many other collections besides his own.
2. A deceased woman who was known for a cardigan-style suit look that still bears her name.
3. A Frenchman who designed elaborate gowns for famous people until his death in 1982.
4. This American designer of the past was the first Coty Award and Coty Hall of Fame winner.
5. This Japanese woman is creative with unconventional designs in neutrals and earthtones.
6. Arnold is a Coty Award winner and does glamorous gowns.
7. Mary works in the United States, creating eccentric designs in decorative fabrics and luxurious evening clothes.
8. This man has the "Polo" logo.
9. This line from Milan is now designed by the originator's sister, Donatella.
10. Issac creates elegant, but comfortable, clothes.
11. This designer from Rome does ladylike, sophisticated fashions in Paris.
12. This British designer uses upholstery fabrics and tapestries in apparel.
13. Milan is where this man used to design only menswear and now also does unstructured designs with relaxed refinement for women.
14. Claire did elegant sportswear from the late 1930s into the 1950s.
15. This Frenchman creates glamorous evening wear and ladies' suits and dresses with perfection of cut and lasting quality.
16. Italian design family who creates multicolored knitwear.
17. Liz's firm is well-known for comfortable, fashionable clothes, especially for working women.
18. This designer in Florence uses the "GG" logo.
19. Claude sometimes has far-out designs with strong silhouette, color, and texture.
20. This Filipino designer creates conservative, elegant gowns.
21. Emanuel is known for sensuously draped dresses and loud prints and textures.
22. Bill is a Coty Hall of Fame winner who does stylish, wearable, elegant clothes.

Characteristic Work of Designers

Name _____

Date _____ Period_____

Cut out pictures of garments from two well-known designers and mount them here. Then explain why the garments you chose are characteristic of the work of those designers. (Consider the types of clothes, colors, fabrics, etc.)

1. These garments are characteristic of the work of

designer _____

because _____

_____

_____

_____

_____

_____

_____

2. These garments are characteristic of the work of

designer _____

because _____

_____

_____

_____

_____

_____

_____

Extending Your Knowledge of Designers

Activity D

Chapter 4

Name _____

Date _____ Period_____

In a current magazine or newspaper, read about a designer (preferably someone new on the scene who has not been mentioned in this chapter). Write a brief profile about the designer, including his or her business size and location, characteristic work, relative price range, and clientele.

Designer's name: _____

_____

_____

_____

_____

_____

_____

_____

_____

_____

_____

_____

_____

_____

_____

_____

_____

_____

_____

_____

_____

_____

_____

_____

_____

_____

_____

_____

_____

_____

Fashionable Opinions

Activity E

Chapter 4

Name _____

Date _____ Period_____

Think carefully about the following questions and write your opinion about each on the lines provided. You will not be graded on your opinion but should be able to back it up.

1. How do you feel about the stealing of design ideas within the fashion industry? _____
   _____
   _____
   _____

2. Why do you think most creatively talented designers need financial backers and/or business partners?
   _____
   _____

3. What do you think about the high expenses for couture showings versus the benefits received from them?
   _____
   _____

4. Why do you think so many fashion designers work in countries other than their home nations? Does it
   matter in this international business? _____
   _____
   _____
   _____

5. Why do fashion ideas spread so fast around the world today? _____
   _____
   _____

6. In the United States, designer ready-to-wear collections are called "bridge lines." Why do you think they
   have that name? _____
   _____
   _____
   _____

7. Why do so many top designers have RTW lines in addition to their designer lines? Do you agree with their
   reasoning? _____
   _____
   _____
   _____

8. Do you think fashion awards should receive more publicity than they do, such as being televised like the
   Oscars or Emmys? _____
   _____
   _____

A Fashion Interview

Name _____

Date _____ Period_____

For a mock television talk show, write out six pertinent questions you would ask a fashion expert. This person might be the publisher of a trade journal, a fashion reporter who has just attended the Paris prêt à porter showings, the owner of a successful designer franchise store, etc. Then assume the identity of the fashion expert and gather all of the information you need to answer the questions. Have a friend ask you the questions in front of the class for an exclusive interview!

1. _____
   _____
   _____
   _____
   _____

2. _____
   _____
   _____
   _____
   _____

3. _____
   _____
   _____
   _____
   _____

4. _____
   _____
   _____
   _____
   _____

5. _____
   _____
   _____
   _____
   _____

6. _____
   _____
   _____
   _____

Chapter 5

The Textile Industry
and Home Sewing Patterns

The Production of Fabrics

Activity A

Chapter 5

Name _____

Date _____ Period_____

List and describe the four main steps in the production of finished fabrics.

1. _____: _____

_____

_____

_____

2. _____: _____

_____

_____

_____

3. _____: _____

_____

_____

_____

4. _____: _____

_____

_____

_____

Now pull some "threads" from a scrap of fabric.

Untwist a thread and tape some fibers here.

Tape some threads (yarns) here.

Tape a piece of the fabric here.

Textile and Pattern Term Tree

Name _____

Date _____ Period_____

Read the definitions and write the terms in the corresponding spaces in the potted tree shown here. Each darkened square indicates a space between words.

(Continued)

1. _____ -to-sew patterns are simple to cut out and make.

2. Textile production plants that spin fibers into yarns and/or manufacture fabrics from yarns are called _____.

3. A(n) _____ is a basic pattern, in a company's basic size, used as the basis for creating fashion patterns.

4. The financial worth or accumulated investment cash needed to start, expand, or run a business is called _____.

5. _____, or mechanically accomplished tasks done by automated equipment, will become more widespread in the future.

6. The first full-scale trial garment of a new design is called a(n) _____.

7. Efforts in research and development keep the textile industry's _____ up-to-date to combine with fashion and marketing for successful textile lines.

8. A(n) _____ for a home sewing pattern contains illustrated directions for all cutting and sewing steps.

9. Fabrics that are just off the loom or knitting machine in an unfinished state are called _____ _____.

10. A(n) _____ _____ occurs when a country imports more goods than it exports.

11. A(n) _____ _____ is a pattern made to fit an individual's measurements.

12. _____ · _____ are collections of apparel or commercial patterns that have the endorsements of celebrities.

13. Computer-related procedures and technology are called _____.

14. A textile designer who works on a computer points or writes on a(n) _____ _____ with a hand-held wand.

15. _____ _____ are firms, or individual merchants, that buy or handle greige goods for finishing.

16. Home sewing patterns with several sizes printed together on the same pieces are called _____ _____.

17. _____ _____ look about two years ahead to predict coming trends in colors, textures, silhouettes, and accessories.

18. _____ is the creative, forward-thinking introduction of new ideas.

19. _____ is finding or creating a market for specific goods or services by identifying the customer and determining what products will satisfy the customer's needs.

20. _____ is a scientific process of making garment patterns into larger or smaller sizes.

21. A(n) _____ is an "interlock" sewing machine that duplicates ready-to-wear manufacturing techniques. It overcasts and trims the raw edges of garment parts as they are stitched together.

The Versatility of Textiles

Name _____

Date _____ Period_____

Look through magazines, newspapers, and other publications and notice the many ways textiles are used. Cut out two examples of textiles used in unusual ways and mount them in the spaces below along with descriptions of their uses. Compare and discuss your pictures with those of other class members.

1. Description: _____

_____

_____

_____

2. Description: _____

_____

_____

_____

The Importance of Color

Name _____

Date _____ Period_____

Study current fashion magazines and clothing catalogs to determine the newest fashion colors. Cut out three pictures and mount them in these boxes. Next to each, write your reactions to the color and how it is used. Give its "new" name or names. If it is a modification of a color used last year, give the fashionable name of the "old" color. Predict how long you think the "new" color will remain in fashion. If you think it might be altered slightly for the next season, describe the future color and give it a fashionable name.

1. _____

_____

_____

_____

_____

_____

_____

_____

_____

_____

_____

_____

_____

_____

_____

_____

_____

_____

_____

(Continued)

2. _____
_____
_____
_____
_____
_____
_____
_____
_____
_____
_____
_____
_____
_____
_____

3. _____
_____
_____
_____
_____
_____
_____
_____
_____
_____
_____
_____
_____
_____
_____
_____
_____

Put Your Knowledge to the Test

Activity E

Chapter 5

Name _____

Date _____ Period_____

Prepare a thought-provoking test question and answer for each of the following headings of this chapter.

1. Fabric production and distribution.

   Question: _____

   _____

   Answer: _____

   _____

2. The development of textile corporations.

   Question: _____

   _____

   Answer: _____

   _____

3. Textile technology, fashion, and marketing.

   Question: _____

   _____

   Answer: _____

   _____

4. Textiles worldwide.

   Question: _____

   _____

   Answer: _____

   _____

5. The future of textiles.

   Question: _____

   _____

   Answer: _____

   _____

(Continued)

6. The business of patterns.

   Question: _____

   _____

   Answer: _____

   _____

7. The breadth of pattern companies.

   Question: _____

   _____

   Answer: _____

   _____

8. Designing commercial patterns.

   Question: _____

   _____

   Answer: _____

   _____

9. Perfecting the patterns.

   Question: _____

   _____

   Answer: _____

   _____

10. Finishing the patterns.

    Question: _____

    _____

    Answer: _____

    _____

11. Innovations for the future.

    Question: _____

    _____

    Answer: _____

    _____

Tell the Difference

Activity A   Name _____

Chapter 6   Date _____ Period_____

What is the difference between:

1. Inside shops and outside shops? _____
   _____
   _____
   _____

2. Samples and samplings? _____
   _____
   _____
   _____

3. Designers and stylists? _____
   _____
   _____
   _____

4. CAD, CAM, and CIM? _____
   _____
   _____
   _____

5. Marker and spreader? _____
   _____
   _____
   _____

6. Piecework system and tailor system?_____
   _____
   _____
   _____

(Continued)

7. Progressive bundle system and unit production system? _____

_____

_____

_____

8. Modular manufacturing and section construction? _____

_____

_____

_____

9. Merchandising and benchmarking? _____

_____

_____

_____

10. Ergonomics and productivity? _____

_____

_____

_____

11. Quick Response and (TC)^2? _____

_____

_____

_____

12. Offshore production and domestic production? _____

_____

_____

_____

13. Lead time and response time? _____

_____

_____

_____

Working as a Designer and a Stylist

Name _____

Date _____ Period_____

On one of the two figures drawn here, design a garment from a specific source of inspiration. Next to it, mount a picture, advertisement, or news clipping indicating the source of your idea for the design. Describe the association between the source of inspiration and your design.

On the other figure, redesign a garment by adapting an existing fashion. Next to it, mount a picture of the garment you changed. Describe what changes you made and why.

1. _____

_____

_____

_____

_____

_____

_____

_____

(Continued)

Name _____

2. _____

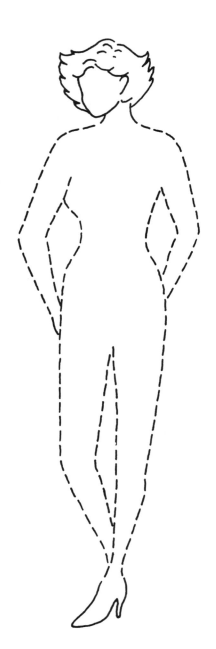

Personal Reactions

Name _____

Date _____ Period_____

Think about the following statements and write your reaction to each on the lines provided.

1. Fashion designers often know by "gut feel" what to create if they stay aware of social, financial, and cultural happenings. _____

   _____

   _____

   _____

   _____

2. More and more firms are constructing apparel by supplementing traditional operations with robots and vision systems, computer-controlled conveyors, and stitchless joining. _____

   _____

   _____

   _____

   _____

3. Since about 75 percent of a tailored clothing operator's time is spent accepting, aligning, and transferring the work (rather than sewing), automation of the "material handling" aspect of production is crucial to improving the efficiency and profitability of tailored clothing companies. _____

   _____

   _____

   _____

   _____

4. Many experts say that the U.S. apparel production industry should try to revitalize itself with more flexibility and better management rather than with government trade legislation and offshore production.

   _____

   _____

   _____

   _____

5. Some apparel manufacturers are advertising directly to consumers to create a customer demand that "pulls" retailers to buy their items rather than just "pushing" their lines directly to retailers through sales reps and market week showings._____

   _____

   _____

   _____

   _____

Apparel Production Terms

Name _____

Date _____ Period_____

Complete the sentences by writing the correct term in each blank.

1. In garment manufacturing, a(n) _____ is a long piece of paper that has a drawing of the layout of all the pattern pieces for cutting.

2. A limitation established by the government on the quantity of a certain category of goods that can enter the country during a particular time span is called a(n) _____.

3. _____ is a procedure done to figure the expenses of producing something, such as a garment of a new design.

4. In the future, CAD will enable computer _____ to show a sketch in three dimensions from any angle so all sides of a fashion design can be seen.

5. A fashion _____ redesigns existing garments into knock-offs, rather than creating new fashion designs.

6. _____ is the incoming money that is left over in a business after all the outgoing costs have been deducted.

7. The manufacturing of goods in one's own country, such as the United States, is called _____ production.

8. An example of a(n) _____ venture is the partnership of a domestic and foreign producer for production and sales overseas.

9. When a master pattern is _____, all of its pieces are made into larger and smaller sizes.

10. The shortened term for a computer system that uses electronics for the production of apparel is _____.

11. A(n) _____ is a commercial product sent out of the country to other countries.

12. _____ time is the amount of time between the placing of an order for merchandise and the desired delivery date.

13. Small quantities of garments placed in retail stores to get an indication of consumer reaction to them are called _____.

14. A(n) _____ is a style or design that is produced at the same time by many different manufacturers at many different prices.

15. The shortened term for a computer system used to combine and visualize ideas and to make patterns and prepare them for cutting is _____.

16. The use of automated equipment to do mechanically accomplished tasks with little or no human intervention is known as _____.

(Continued)

17. A fringe _____ is extra compensation, other than pay, such as vacation time, insurance, and sick leave.

18. A manufacturer who does any or all of the cutting, sewing, and finishing work for other apparel producers under a contractual arrangement is called a(n) _____.

19. The _____ system is a manufacturing procedure in which one specific task is done by each person along an assembly line.

20. _____ production is manufacturing that is done overseas.

21. Goods that come into the country from foreign sources are _____.

22. The abbreviation for a production system that combines CAD, CAM, robotics, and company information systems is _____.

23. The abbreviation for a computerized apparel manufacturing system that uses an overhead product carrier to move garment pieces along is _____.

24. _____ Response is a textile-apparel-retail business strategy that ties together all of the pipeline parts as one unified industry rather than as individual segments.

25. _____ is the process through which products are designed, developed, and promoted to the point of sale.

26. Sometimes called human engineering, _____ matches human performance to the tasks being done, the equipment used, and the environment.

27. Higher _____ results from using resources more efficiently and effectively, so more output results in relation to the amount of input.

28. The abbreviation $(TC)^2$ stands for the Textile/Clothing _____ Corporation.

29. Modular manufacturing divides the apparel production employees into independent _____or work groups.

30. _____ are trial garments made up exactly as they are intended to look when sold.

31. The _____ system, which is not used much to produce apparel commercially anymore, uses one person to do all the sewing tasks for a garment.

32. When an innovative idea is noticed at one company, it is used as a(n) _____ for other companies to measure their products, services, or practices against.

33. Interactive _____ are now being used with computer text and graphics as portable "tutors" to train industry mechanics and operators.

34. _____ benefits for employees include vacation time and health insurance.

Analyzing Fashion Designs

Name _____

Date _____ Period_____

Clip pictures of four garments from an advertisement, fashion magazine, or clothing catalog. Mount them in the spaces provided below. On the lines beside each box, describe your thoughts about their design and production by answering the following questions. What was the design influence? For what target market (age, income level, etc.) was each garment produced? Was factory production easy or difficult for various parts of the garments? For what season's line were the garments produced? Were the garments made by the piecework, tailor, or other system?

1. _____

_____

_____

_____

_____

_____

_____

_____

_____

_____

_____

_____

2. _____

_____

_____

_____

_____

_____

_____

_____

_____

_____

_____

_____

_____

Name _____

3. _____
   _____
   _____
   _____
   _____
   _____
   _____
   _____
   _____
   _____
   _____
   _____

4. _____
   _____
   _____
   _____
   _____
   _____
   _____
   _____
   _____
   _____
   _____
   _____
   _____
   _____
   _____
   _____

Fashion Promotion and Retailing

Fill-in-the-Blanks

Activity A

Chapter 7

Name _____

Date _____ Period_____

Putting one letter in each blank, write the correct term for each definition below.

1. _ _ _ _ _ _ _ _ _ _ _ is indirect, or nonpersonal, selling aimed at a large general audience.

2. The business of selling merchandise directly to consumers is called _ _ _ _ _ _ _ _ _ _.

3. A(n) _ _ _ _ _ _ _ _ _ _ _ _ is a low-priced article that is intended to attract shoppers into a store rather than to generate a profit.

4. _ _ _ _ _ _ control is the receiving, storing, and distributing of merchandise in a retail store.

5. _ _ _ _ _ _ _ _ _ _ _ _ is store merchandise that is constantly in demand and stocked continuously.

6. A(n) _ _ _ _ _ _ _ _ _ _ _ _ _ _ _ is a written document, made out by the buyer, authorizing a seller to deliver certain goods at specified prices.

7. A(n) _ _ _ _ _ _ _ is an incomplete assortment of goods bought by a retailer at a reduced price and used as a source of sale items.

8. _ _ _ _ _ _ _ stores provide the attraction needed to draw customers to shopping malls.

9. _ _ _ _ _-_ _-_ _ _is the amount of merchandise that buyers are permitted to order during a specified time period.

10. _ _ _-_ _ _ _ _ _ _ _ _ _ _ _ _ _ _ _ _ _ are stores that carry well- known brand name merchandise at lower than normal prices.

11. _ _ _ _ _ _ _ _ _ _ _ _ _ _ _ are small retail outlets with a wide assortment of lower-priced merchandise displayed on open counters.

12. Web-based retailing, done electronically via the Internet, is referred to as " _-_ _ _ _ _ _ _ _."

13. Merchandise tags now contain bar codes, so electronic _ _ _ _ _ _ _ _ _ can automatically record inventory and point-of-sale data into the computer system.

14. A(n) _ _ _ _ _ _ _ department is space within a store operated by an outside firm, such as shoes.

15. A(n) _ _ _ _ _ _ _ _ _ _ _ store handles a specific kind of merchandise or one category of goods, such as children's wear.

Noticing Private Labels

Name _____

Date _____ Period_____

1. Define private label merchandise: _____

   _____

   _____

   _____

   _____

   _____

2. From shopping in stores or from reading advertisements or catalogs, write down four private label brand names and the stores, or groups of stores, that own them.

Private Label	Store
_____	_____
_____	_____
_____	_____
_____	_____

3. From catalogs or advertisements, cut out two pictures of private label garments. Attach them to this page. For each, describe the type of store that owns the label and list other items that have the same label. Also compare the price and quality of each garment to a similar garment with a well-known manufacturer's label.

   A. _____

   _____

   _____

   _____

   _____

   _____

   _____

   _____

   _____

   B. _____

   _____

   _____

   _____

   _____

   _____

   _____

   _____

   _____

   _____

Differences Described

Name _____

Date _____ Period_____

What is the difference between:

1. Direct and indirect selling? _____

_____

_____

_____

2. Advertising and publicity? _____

_____

_____

_____

3. Visual merchandising and video merchandising? _____

_____

_____

_____

4. Markup and markdown? _____

_____

_____

_____

5. Odd-figure pricing and package pricing? _____

_____

_____

_____

6. Completion date and as ready? _____

_____

_____

_____

7. Flagship store and branch store? _____

_____

_____

_____

8. Chains and franchises?_____

_____

_____

_____

(Continued)

Name _____

9. Mail-order retailing and telecommunication retailing? _____
_____
_____
_____

10. Offshore sourcing and commissionaires? _____
_____
_____
_____

11. Product developers and private label? _____
_____
_____
_____

12. Margin and profit? _____
_____
_____
_____

13. Resident buying services and regional marts? _____
_____
_____
_____

14. Discount stores and factory outlets? _____
_____
_____
_____

15. Shoppertainment and niche retailing? _____
_____
_____
_____

16. Television retailing and computer retailing? _____
_____
_____
_____

Statements of Interest

Name _____

Date _____ Period_____

Read the following statements and give your reaction to each. Check if you think the statement is an interesting aspect of fashion promotion and sales, if it seems uninteresting to you, or if you are unsure about your feelings toward it. You will not be graded on your responses. Then choose what you feel the most interesting statement of the group is and explain your reaction to it in detail.

Interesting   Uninteresting   Unsure

_____   _____   _____   1. An "assortment plan" is usually compiled by a buyer of a category of merchandise for a store with branches. The plan indicates what styles, colors, and sizes are allotted to each branch store.

_____   _____   _____   2. "Infomercials" are 5- to 60- minute commercially provided video tapes. They inform people of the latest fashion trends while advertising in a subtle way.

_____   _____   _____   3. The role of retailers is becoming more powerful in influencing trends and fashion industry issues. This is because many firms are expanding into all areas of supply, production, and sales to become "multifaceted" or "vertically integrated" businesses.

_____   _____   _____   4. Most fashion retailers subscribe to the Fashion Calendar®, which gives dates and locations of fashion showings, market weeks, and important industry events around the world.

_____   _____   _____   5. Stock keeping units (SKUs) are the smallest unit for which sales and stock records are kept for retail control and identification purposes. Computerized UPC/scanner systems are absolutely necessary, since large department stores might have two million SKUs to monitor!

_____   _____   _____   6. Sometimes retail store markdown racks of slow-selling apparel actually contain fashions that will be popular next season. Buyers may have pushed the items too early.

_____   _____   _____   7. When one well-established retail firm computerized, the data showed that more short inseam men's pants were sold downtown and more long inseam pants were sold in the suburbs. The computer information indicated the need to stock the downtown store with pants for smaller, older men and the suburban stores with pants for younger, taller customers.

_____   _____   _____   8. The nation's highest volume fashion department store emphasizes quality customer service rather than advertising. Salespeople, considered the company's most valuable asset, go out of their way to please customers. They may specially order merchandise, lower prices to match those of competitors, or have items delivered by taxi follow telephone orders.

(Continued)

Interesting   Uninteresting   Unsure

_____   _____   _____   9. Bureaucratic structures (too many levels of management) have added to the large overhead costs of many department stores. Now they are having financial difficulties and cannot pay salaries and benefits. The stores are being forced to have fewer levels of management for a "flatter, meaner, and leaner" hierarchy.

_____   _____   _____   10. People used to have extra time to shop just for fun. Now people are too busy to shop and their lifestyles have changed—they want more casual clothes than before, and prefer to relax at home if they find spare time. Consumer attitudes have changed and retailers cannot do anything about it.

_____   _____   _____   11. Video walls made up of many television screens are stimulating fashion interest in retail stores and malls. The image on each screen is coordinated with the others to either form separate pictures, combine pictures forming sections of the wall, or form one big picture with each monitor showing a fraction of the total image.

_____   _____   _____   12. Even though video merchandising has not been as successful as anticipated for promotion, merchandise videos effectively teach sales personnel about the newest products and latest selling techniques. They are cost-effective, since they can be played over and over when desired.

_____   _____   _____   13. Much of the time and money spent shopping for pleasure and psychological satisfaction has been replaced by eating at restaurants or watching movies.

_____   _____   _____   14. Many retailers are alike, but customers have individual tastes and preferences. Shoppers find an oversupply of basic merchandise but an undersupply of unique, focused items.

_____   _____   _____   15. Mail-order catalogs that look like fashion magazines and contain some articles are called "magalogs." Other catalogs have personalized messages for each household receiving them, such as family names and crests on merchandise. Some catalogs have entertaining storytelling copy.

My favorite statement is #_____ because _____

_____

_____

_____

_____

_____

_____

_____

_____

Retail Outlets

Name _____

Date _____ Period_____

Answer the questions below. Then complete the exercise that follows. Use a separate sheet of paper to record your responses if necessary.

1. Retail site: Think about what stores you, your family, and your friends shop in because of location. Analyze how important you think the location of a store is to its success. Write your opinion and any examples you can think of here: _____

    _____

    _____

2. Image: Think about several stores that portray different images, or impressions, to the public. Analyze their interior decor, number and type of salespeople, labels, prices, promotional activities, policies, and services offered. Write your analysis here: _____

    _____

    _____

3. Merchandise mix: Think about the variety of products offered in different stores. Does the merchandise seem to be aimed at a target market or does it try to satisfy all types of people? Is there too little or too much merchandise? Is the merchandise consistent with the store's location and image? Write your analysis here: _____

    _____

    _____

Now compare two different retail outlets in your area.

4. Name of store: _____

    Type of retail outlet: _____

    Retail site/location: _____

    Image: _____

    Merchandise mix: _____

    The store's strong points: _____

    The store's weak points: _____

    Recommendations for improvements: _____

    _____

5. Name of store: _____

    Type of retail outlet: _____

    Retail site/location: _____

    Image: _____

    Merchandise mix: _____

    The store's strong points: _____

    The store's weak points: _____

    Recommendations for improvements: _____

    _____

From Beginning to End

Name _____

Date _____ Period_____

Define "channel of distribution." _____

_____

_____

After reviewing the channel of distribution shown on page 104 of the textbook, study the more detailed version here below.

The apparel channel of distribution, sometimes called the "textile/apparel pipeline," or the "soft goods chain," ties together all of the information in Chapters 4 through 7 of this text. Write a paragraph using all of the identified subheadings of the textile/apparel pipeline shown below. Describe the process from beginning to end for an article of clothing, such as a shirt, dress, or pants.

_____   *Textile segment* {
_____   — Fiber production
_____   — Yarn production
_____   — Fabric manufacturing
_____   — Fabric finishing
_____   *Apparel segment* {
_____   — Apparel designing
_____   — Apparel manufacturing
_____   — Wholesale apparel selling
_____   *Retail segment* {
_____   — Quantity buying
_____   — Single-item selling
_____
_____   *End Users*   *Consumers*
_____

_____

_____

_____

_____

_____

_____

_____

Textile Fibers and Yarns

Fiber Facts

Activity A   Name _____

Chapter 8   Date _____ Period_____

This is a two-part activity. First complete the following statements about fibers and unscramble the circled letters to spell a related term. Then complete the activity that follows.

1. Fibers, such as cotton, linen, rayon, acetate, and triacetate, are derived from plants and are called
   _ _ _ _ ⭕ _ _ _ _ _ fibers.

2. _ _ _ _ _ _ ⭕ fibers, such as silk, wool, and specialty hair fibers, are of animal origin.

3. The process of cleaning and straightening staple fibers by a machine with a series of rollers of various
   sizes with fine wire teeth is called _ _ _ _ ⭕ _ _.

4. An additional step in processing that further straightens long, high-quality staple fibers is called
   _ _ _ ⭕ _ _ _.

5. _ _ ⭕ _ _ _ _ is the process of pulling laps, slivers, or rovings to blend the fibers, arrange them in
   parallel order, and increase uniformity.

6. The natural fiber linen is obtained from the ⭕ _ _ _ plant.

7. _ _ _ ⭕ _ _ _ yarns are made from long wool fibers that have been combed.

8. _ _ _ _ ⭕ _ _ _ wool refers to wool fibers from previously made wool fabrics.

9. A(n) _ _ _ _ _ ⭕ _ _ _ is a long, fine, continuous thread that is extruded by a fiber manufacturer or
   found naturally as silk.

10. The science of raising silkworms for the production of silk fibers is called _ _ ⭕ _ _ _ _ _ _ _ _.

11. _ _ _ _ _ _ _ ⭕ are chemical compounds from which many manufactured fibers are made.

12. A(n) _ _ _ ⭕ _ _ _ name is given to each group of manufactured fibers that are of similar
    chemical composition.

13. To make manufactured fibers, the raw materials are converted into a liquid state and then
    _ _ _ _ ⭕ _ _ or forced through openings.

14. When describing fiber diameter, the higher the ⭕ _ _ _ _ _, the thicker the fiber.

15. A(n) _ _ _ _ _ ⭕ _ _ _ is a metal disc containing many tiny holes through which the liquid
    fiber-forming solution is forced to form manufactured filaments.

16. Short fibers of various lengths from natural sources or cut lengths of manufactured fibers are called
    _ _ ⭕ _ _ _.

(Continued)

17. Large, continuous filament bundles of manufactured fibers are called ( )_ _.

18. _ _ _ _ _( )_ _ _ is a filling material made of crimped, staple manufactured fibers that are not made into yarns.

Circled letters: _

Unscramble the letters to spell the term:

_ _ _ _ _ _ _ _ _ _ _ _ _   _ _ _ _ _ _

(Clue: The term can be used to complete this sentence: In this chapter, we learned about natural and

_____ _____ as well as yarns.)

Based on your knowledge of manufactured fibers, match the procedures for producing nylon fibers on the left to the corresponding blanks on the right. Numbers 1, 4, and 7 have been done for you.

Procedures

Cooling

Winding onto spools

Melter

Polymer chips

Spinneret

Stretching

Twisting

1. Solid, synthetic polyamid materials

2. _____

3. _____

4. Extruder

5. _____

6. _____

7. Monofilament wind-up

8. _____

9. _____

10. _____

A Spool of Fibers

Name _____

Date _____ Period_____

Draw a "thread" from each definition on the right to the correct fiber listed on the spool at the left. Then complete the activities at the bottom of the page.

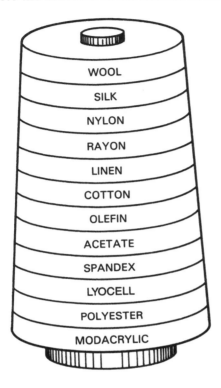

WOOL
SILK
NYLON
RAYON
LINEN
COTTON
OLEFIN
ACETATE
SPANDEX
LYOCELL
POLYESTER
MODACRYLIC

1. This strong fiber was the first to be manufactured totally from chemicals.
2. This stretchy fiber is strong, lightweight, and durable.
3. This fiber of regenerated cellulose was the first one to be commercially manufactured.
4. This fiber is obtained from cocoons spun by worms.
5. This most widely used manufactured fiber is strong, wrinkle-resistant, and often blended with other fibers for easy care.
6. This fiber is manufactured from cellulose acetate.
7. This fiber is obtained from the stalk of the flax plant.
8. This fiber is obtained from the fleece of sheep.
9. This popular fiber comes from the boll of a plant.
10. This manufactured fiber is used extensively for flame retardant sleepwear and also for furlike fabrics.
11. This fiber, often called polyproplyene, has good wicking power.
12. This environmentally friendly fiber is manufactured with wood pulp from trees grown in managed, replanted forests.

List the fiber names from the spool under the correct category:

Natural fibers	**Manufactured cellulosic fibers**	**Manufactured noncellulosic fibers**
_____	_____	_____
_____	_____	_____
_____	_____	_____
_____	_____	_____
_____	_____	_____

Review glossary definitions and chapter information about woolens and worsteds. Then label the two sections of this drawing according to what is most representative of each.

_____   _____

Chapter Content Clues

Activity C

Activity C   Name _____

Chapter 8   Date _____ Period_____

This is a two-part activity. In the blank next to each number below, write the letter *N* if the written "clue" relates to natural fibers, the letter *M* if it relates to manufactured fibers, or the letter *Y* if it relates to yarns. Then complete the exercises at the bottom of the page.

_____	1. Specialty wools	_____	8. Aramid	_____	15. Ply
_____	2. Variants	_____	9. Sericin	_____	16. Anidex
_____	3. Dry spinning	_____	10. Multifilament	_____	17. Solution dyeing
_____	4. Mechanical spinning	_____	11. Wet spinning	_____	18. Cord
_____	5. Chemical spinning	_____	12. Spun silk	_____	19. Vinyon
_____	6. Bast	_____	13. Spun yarns	_____	20. Melt spinning
_____	7. Triacetate	_____	14. Tussah	_____	21. Scutching

Give the correct response to the following items.

Natural Fibers

22. Using the glossary in the textbook, write definitions for the following two words:

   A. Staple fibers: _____

      _____

   B. Filament fibers: _____

      _____

23. Explain why all natural fibers except silk are staple fibers. _____

    _____

    _____

    _____

Manufactured Fibers

24. Explain how the use of spandex fibers in apparel has changed recently.

    _____

    _____

    _____

    _____

Yarns

25. What is the difference between monofilament fibers and monofilament yarns? _____

    _____

26. What is the difference between multifilament yarns and spun yarns? _____

    _____

    _____

Generic Names and Trademarks

Activity D

Chapter 8

Name _____

Date _____ Period_____

Complete the following exercises.

1. Define *generic* name. _____

_____

_____

2. Define *variant*. _____

_____

_____

3. Define *trademark*. _____

_____

_____

Match the generic names listed on the left with the trademarks of their variants listed on the right. Put the letter of each variant trademark on the line next to the correct generic name.

Generic Names	**Trademarks**		
4. Acetate. _____	A. Dacron.	K. Marvess.	U. Alpha.
5. Acrylic. _____	B. Estron.	L. PBI.	V. Fibro.
6. Aramid. _____	C. Nomex.	M. Lycra.	W. Kevlar.
7. Lyocell. _____	D. Sayelle.	N. Suplex.	X. Hollofil.
8. Nylon._____	E. Cordura.	O. Micronesse.	Y. Ultron.
9. Olefin._____	F. Tencel.	P. Clearspan.	Z. Herculon.
10. Polybenzimidazole. _____	G. Eco Spun	Q. Fortrel.	
11. Polyester. _____	H. Creslan.	R. Acrilan.	
12. Rayon._____	I. Galaxy.	S. Antron.	
13. Spandex._____	J. Chromspun.	T. Duraspun.	

14. Define *denier*. _____

_____

_____

15. Define *microdenier*. _____

_____

_____

16. Using the chart on pages 141-142 of the textbook, find four trademarks that indicate the fibers are microdeniers.

    A. _____   C. _____

    B. _____   D. _____

Fiber Uses

Activity E

Chapter 8

Name _____

Date _____ Period_____

For each fiber listed, suggest both a satisfactory and an unsatisfactory apparel use and explain your reasoning.

1. Cotton _____

   Satisfactory apparel use: _____

   Reasons: _____

   _____

   Unsatisfactory apparel use: _____

   Reasons: _____

   _____

2. Linen

   Satisfactory apparel use: _____

   Reasons: _____

   _____

   Unsatisfactory apparel use: _____

   Reasons: _____

   _____

3. Wool

   Satisfactory apparel use: _____

   _____

   Reasons: _____

   _____

   Unsatisfactory apparel use: _____

   Reasons: _____

   _____

4. Silk

   Satisfactory apparel use: _____

   Reasons: _____

   _____

   Unsatisfactory apparel use: _____

   Reasons: _____

   _____

(Continued)

5. Polyester

Satisfactory apparel use: _____

Reasons: _____

_____

Unsatisfactory apparel use: _____

Reasons: _____

_____

6. Nylon

Satisfactory apparel use: _____

Reasons: _____

_____

Unsatisfactory apparel use: _____

Reasons: _____

_____

7. Acrylic

Satisfactory apparel use: _____

Reasons: _____

_____

Unsatisfactory apparel use: _____

Reasons: _____

_____

8. Rayon

Satisfactory apparel use: _____

Reasons: _____

_____

Unsatisfactory apparel use: _____

Reasons: _____

_____

9. Acetate

Satisfactory apparel use: _____

Reasons: _____

_____

Unsatisfactory apparel use: _____

Reasons: _____

_____

(Continued)

10. Olefin

Satisfactory apparel use: _____

Reasons: _____

_____

Unsatisfactory apparel use: _____

Reasons: _____

_____

11. Spandex

Satisfactory apparel use: _____

Reasons: _____

_____

Unsatisfactory apparel use: _____

Reasons: _____

_____

12. Lyocell

Satisfactory apparel use: _____

Reasons: _____

_____

Unsatisfactory apparel use: _____

Reasons:_____

_____

13. Aramid

Satisfactory apparel use: _____

Reasons: _____

_____

Unsatisfactory apparel use: _____

Reasons: _____

_____

14. Polybenzimidazole

Satisfactory apparel use: _____

Reasons: _____

_____

Unsatisfactory apparel use: _____

Reasons: _____

_____

Fabric Construction and Finishes

Practice with Fabric Construction

Activity A

Chapter 9

Name _____

Date _____ Period_____

From a skein of knitting yarn, cut 72 pieces, each 3 inches long. In each of these three boxes, tape the ends of 12 pieces to the left sides and bottoms as indicated. Then weave the yarns to create samples of a plain weave, a twill weave, and a satin weave.

In the boxes on the next page, mount, name, and describe fabric samples of a weft knit, a warp knit, and another construction method.

Tape 12 Ends

Tape 12 Ends

Plain Weave

Tape 12 Ends

Tape 12 Ends

Twill Weave

Tape 12 Ends

Tape 12 Ends

Satin Weave

(Continued)

Construction: Weft Knit

Fabric name: _____

Description: _____

_____

_____

_____

_____

Construction: Warp Knit

Fabric name: _____

Description: _____

_____

_____

_____

_____

Construction: _____

Fabric name: _____

Description: _____

_____

_____

_____

_____

Fabric Construction Terms

Name _____

Date _____ Period_____

Match the following terms with their definitions.

_____ 1. The strong lengthwise edges of fabric that do not ravel.

_____ 2. A machine for weaving fabric.

_____ 3. The yarns that run along the lengthwise grain of woven fabrics.

_____ 4. Lines of loops that run the length of knitted fabrics.

_____ 5. Permanently fastening together two layers of fabric.

_____ 6. A stretchy knit fabric constructed on a single needle, weft knitting machine.

_____ 7. The number of stitches, or loops, per inch in a knitted fabric.

_____ 8. The portion of a yarn that extends for some length without being woven or knitted back into the fabric construction.

_____ 9. A variation of the plain weave.

_____10. A thick, somewhat stiff type of nonwoven fabric that can be molded into shapes.

_____11. Fabrics knit with one continuous strand of yarn that forms horizontal rows of interlocked loops.

_____12. A basic fabric weave that has long yarn floats on the surface that produce a smooth, lustrous appearance.

_____13. Loops or yarn ends that project out from a fabric's surface.

_____14. The fabric grain that runs diagonally across the fabric.

_____15. The yarns that run along the crosswise grain of woven fabrics.

_____16. Fabrics that are made directly from fibers rather than from yarns.

_____17. Simplest and most common weave in which filling yarns pass alternately over and under warp yarns.

_____18. A basic fabric weave characterized by diagonal wales.

_____19. The fabric grain that is formed by the filling yarns.

_____20. A machine that weaves large, intricate designs using a series of programmed punch cards; now computerized.

_____21. Fabrics made on flat knitting machines using many yarns and needles, with interlocking loops in the lengthwise direction.

_____22. A layer of raised fiber ends that changes in appearance when viewed from different directions.

_____23. Rows of loops or stitches running across a knit fabric.

_____24. The fabric grain that is formed by the warp yarns.

_____25. A fabric produced on a weft knitting machine with two sets of needles and yarns that knit two fabrics as one.

_____26. A variation of the twill weave in which the wale changes direction at regular intervals to produce a zigzag effect.

A. basket weave

B. bias grain

C. bonding

D. courses

E. crosswise grain

F. double knit

G. felt

H. filling yarns

I. float

J. gauge

K. herringbone

L. jacquard loom

M. lengthwise grain

N. loom

O. nap

P. nonwovens

Q. pile

R. plain weave

S. satin weave

T. selvages

U. single knit

V. twill weave

W. wales

X. warp knits

Y. warp yarns

Z. weft knits

Fabric Coloring and Printing Crossword

Activity C

Chapter 9

Name _____

Date _____ Period_____

Complete the crossword puzzle using the clues listed.

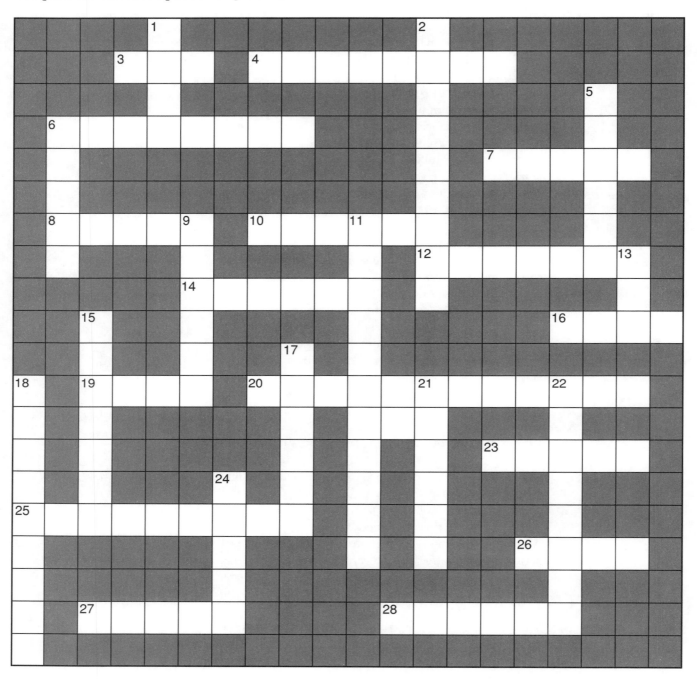

(Continued)

Across:

3. The colorfast dyes that are used in a piece dyeing method used mainly with cellulosic fibers.

4. _____dyeing adds color to the fiber material before it is extruded, making the dye a structural part of the fibers.

6. A process for adding color, pattern, or design to the surface of fabrics.

7. _____dyeing imparts color to fibers before they are spun into yarns.

8. _____dyeing produces two or more colors at once in cases where fibers with different dyeing properties are combined in a fabric.

10. A print that has a distinct design on just part of the fabric, usually along one or both sides.

12. In_____dyeing, clothes (especially knitted ones) are manufactured using undyed yarns. When specific orders are received, the clothes are dyed and then shipped.

14. _____printing is a simple, high-speed process that is sometimes called direct, calender, or cylinder printing.

16. Natural or synthetic substances that give color to textiles.

19. A balanced or_____plaid is the same in both the lengthwise and crosswise directions.

20. _____ _____printing is done by transferring the design onto fabric from preprinted paper by applying heat and pressure.

23. In_____printing, the raised part of a carved design is inked and then placed onto fabric by hand.

25. A term that implies that the color in a fabric will not fade or change with laundering, dry cleaning, or time and use.

26. _____screening is a printing process in which each color requires a separate flat stretched screen made of a sheer fabric.

27. The dyeing of natural fibers in staple form.

28. The method of giving overall color to a fiber, yarn, fabric, or garment.

Down:

1. _____dyeing is done by placing yarns into a dye bath after they have been wound onto spools.

2. _____printing removes dye from certain areas that usually results in a white design on a colored background.

5. This plaid has crossing lines and spaces that are different in one or both directions.

6. _____dyeing is the most common and least expensive method of coloring textiles.

9. _____printing is a high-quality printing method similar to stenciling.

11. A(n)_____print has a specific up and down direction.

13. _____dyeing is a form of resist dyeing using tight fabric folds to form barriers to the dye where desired.

15. A(n)_____print is a design that is the same across all of a piece of fabric.

17. In_____dyeing, areas to be colored are exposed to the dye, while areas that are not to be colored are restricted from the dye.

18. A chemical process that removes color and impurities from fibers or fabrics during finishing.

21. _____screen printing is a combination of roller and screen printing in which dye is pushed through a porous cylindrical screen to apply each color.

22. A method of cloth ornamentation in which finely chopped fibers are sprinkled onto a glue substance for a textured design pattern.

24. A type of resist dyeing that uses wax to cover areas where dye is not wanted.

Fabric Knowledge

Name _____

Date _____ Period_____

Obtain six fabric samples and mount them in the boxes. Unravel a corner of each sample. Indicate the type of weave or knit and whether the fabric has been dyed or printed.

1. _____

2. _____

3. _____

4. _____

5. _____

6. _____

Fabric Finishes Scramble

Activity E

Chapter 9

Name _____

Date _____ Period_____

Unscramble the letters to identify types of fabric finishes.

1. NAEREDNLIGC __ __ __ __ __ __ __ __ __ __ __

   Passing fabric between heated rollers to produce special effects.

2. TGUICTN __ __ __ __ __ __ __

   Done for some napped fabrics, such as corduroy, to create a cut pile.

3. IEAHGNRS __ __ __ __ __ __ __ __

   Trims any fiber or yarn ends that are sticking out from the fabric.

4. YGRNDI DAN ITHNSGRCET __ __ __ __ __ __ __ __ __ __ __ __ __ __ __ __ __ __ __

   General term for the finishing processes called heat setting, crabbing, and tentering.

5. LEBTENGI __ __ __ __ __ __ __ __

   Pounding linen or cotton fabrics to produce a flatter, harder surface with increased sheen.

6. VOPMICRSESE GHRSKIINN __ __ __ __ __ __ __ __ __ __ __ __ __ __ __ __ __ __ __

   A finishing process resulting in a controlled standard of fabric shrinkage of not more than 1 percent.

7. UIRBHNSG __ __ __ __ __ __ __ __

   Pulling up fiber ends from a fabric's surface to produce a soft, fuzzy (napped) finish.

8. NNIIGGES __ __ __ __ __ __ __ __

   Passing fabric over a series of gas jets, a flame, or heated copper plates to remove any protruding fibers.

9. TERAZMIRCIENO __ __ __ __ __ __ __ __ __ __ __ __ __

   A caustic soda treatment for cellulosic textiles to increase the luster, strength, absorbency, and dyeability of the fibers.

10. OSLI EEEALSR __ __ __ __ __ __ __ __ __ __ __

    A chemical finish for fabrics that eases the removal of dirt and stains.

11. CATTTISINA __ __ __ __ __ __ __ __ __ __

    A chemical finish that prevents the buildup of static electricity so garments will not cling.

12. NERPEMATN-SPRSE __ __ __ __ __ __ __ __ __-__ __ __ __ __

    A finish that enables garments to retain their shapes and resist wrinkling during wearing and after laundering.

13. MELAF-STINECSRAE __ __ __ __ __-__ __ __ __ __ __ __ __ __ __

    A finish that prevents fabric from supporting or spreading a flame.

14. WOPOFARETR __ __ __ __ __ __ __ __ __ __

    A finish that fills the pores of a fabric so water cannot pass through it.

15. SREECA-EEITCNRSS __ __ __ __ __ __-__ __ __ __ __ __ __ __ __ __

    A finish that helps fabrics, especially cottons, rayons, and linens, resist and recover from wrinkles.

Identifying Fabrics

Name _____

Date _____ Period_____

Define the following methods of making fabrics:

1. Weaving: _____
   _____
   _____

2. Knitting: _____
   _____
   _____

3. Felting: _____
   _____
   _____

4. Bonding: _____
   _____
   _____

Look at the following list of fabrics. If a fabric is of woven construction, write *W* in the blank to the left of the number. If the fabric is knitted, write *K* in the blank. To the right of each fabric, name the type of weave (plain, twill, or satin) or the type of knit (weft or warp) used to produce it.

_____ 5. Chiffon. _____	_____ 25. Ninon. _____
_____ 6. Double knit. _____	_____ 26. Jersey. _____
_____ 7. Cambric. _____	_____ 27. Denim. _____
_____ 8. Interlock. _____	_____ 28. Monk's cloth. _____
_____ 9. Tricot. _____	_____ 29. Serge. _____
_____ 10. Madras. _____	_____ 30. Nainsook. _____
_____ 11. Covert cloth. _____	_____ 31. Chino. _____
_____ 12. Batiste. _____	_____ 32. Pongee. _____
_____ 13. Challis. _____	_____ 33. Herringbone. _____
_____ 14. Homespun. _____	_____ 34. Matte jersey. _____
_____ 15. Satin. _____	_____ 35. Lawn. _____
_____ 16. Oxford cloth. _____	_____ 36. Sateen. _____
_____ 17. Muslin. _____	_____ 37. Surah. _____
_____ 18. Chintz. _____	_____ 38. Organdy. _____
_____ 19. Burlap. _____	_____ 39. Hopsacking. _____
_____ 20. Chambray. _____	_____ 40. Cavalry twill. _____
_____ 21. Gabardine. _____	_____ 41. Duck. _____
_____ 22. Canvas. _____	_____ 42. Percale. _____
_____ 23. Middy twill. _____	_____ 43. Shantung. _____
_____ 24. Taffeta. _____	_____ 44. Raschel. _____

Chapter 10 | The Element of Color

Working with Color Schemes

Activity A   Name _____

Chapter 10   Date _____ Period_____

Read the description below. Fill in the letter of the color scheme in the first blank and the letter of the appropriate color combination in the second blank. Describe your favorite color scheme. Then show examples of three color schemes by mounting fabric swatches or pictures of them in the boxes provided.

Color schemes

A.   accented neutral
B.   analogous
C.   complementary
D.   monochromatic
E.   split-complementary
F.   triad

Color combinations

G.   red-orange and blue-green
H.   red-violet, yellow-orange, blue-green
I.   white, gray, violet
J.   yellow, yellow-green, green
K.   violet, yellow-green, yellow-orange
L.   light green, medium green, dark green

Color Scheme	Color Combination	Description
_____	_____	1. A one-color plan that combines different tints, shades, and intensities.
_____	_____	2. A plan that uses three hues evenly spaced around the color wheel.
_____	_____	3. A plan that uses colors that are next to each other on the color wheel.
_____	_____	4. A plan that uses hues located directly across from each other on the color wheel.
_____	_____	5. A plan that uses one color with the two colors on the sides of its complement.
_____	_____	6. A plan that uses a bright hue with one or more neutrals.

Description of my favorite color scheme:_____

_____

(Continued)

Name of color scheme:

_____

Colors used:

_____

_____

_____

Name of color scheme:

_____

Colors used:

_____

_____

_____

Name of color scheme:

_____

Colors used:

_____

_____

_____

Color Fill-In

Activity B

Chapter 10

Name _____

Date _____ Period_____

Fill in the squares with the correct terms.

1. The use of yellow with red-violet and blue-violet is an example of a _____-_____ color scheme.
2. The _____ _____ shows the relationships between colors and can be used as a guide for choosing and combining colors.
3. A color's _____ is its brightness or dullness.
4. _____ hues are made by combining equal amounts of adjoining primary and secondary colors.
5. The _____ of a hue is its lightness or darkness from almost white to almost black.
6. The _____ color scheme uses hues directly across from each other on the color wheel.
7. Red, yellow, and blue are _____ hues.
8. _____ is the name given to a color that distinguishes it from other colors.
9. The _____ _____ color scheme combines white, black, or gray with a bright color accent.
10. Everyone's skin color has an _____ of either blue or yellow.
11. Hues that remind us of water or the sky, such as green, blue, and violet, are called _____ _____.
12. The _____ _____ _____ are color, shape, line, and texture.
13. The _____ color scheme uses different values and intensities of one color.
14. Orange, green, and violet are _____ hues.
15. Hues that remind us of fire or the sun, such as red, orange, and yellow, are called _____ _____.
16. The _____ color scheme uses adjacent colors on the color wheel.
17. Black, white, and gray are _____ rather than true colors.

Using Color for Effect

Activity C

Chapter 10

Name _____

Date _____ Period _____

Respond to the following questions and statements.

1. How do the apparel industries use color to encourage consumers to buy more clothes? _____

   _____

   _____

   _____

2. Do you agree or disagree with the idea that the colors people wear are clues to their personalities? Why?

   _____

   _____

   _____

   _____

3. Describe the feelings warm colors give and the effects they have. _____

   _____

   _____

4. Describe the feelings cool colors give and the effects they have. _____

   _____

   _____

5. What general effect is achieved by using dark, cool, dull colors? _____

   _____

6. What general effect is achieved by using light, warm, bright colors?_____

   _____

7. How do colors seem to change when viewed under different lights? _____

   _____

8. What effect does using a single color for an entire outfit have?_____

   _____

9. What effect do sharply contrasting colors create? _____

   _____

10. What do you think should be the most important factor a person should consider when selecting colors for clothes: current fashion, body size and shape, favorite colors, or "best" colors based on personal coloring? Why? _____

   _____

   _____

   _____

   _____

Flattering Personal Coloring

Activity D

Chapter 10

Name _____

Date _____ Period _____

Complete the exercises below.

1. What is personal coloring? _____

_____

2. Give a synopsis of the seasonal color approach by summarizing each of the following categories:

A. Winter: _____

_____

_____

_____

_____

_____

_____

B. Spring: _____

_____

_____

_____

_____

_____

_____

_____

C. Summer: _____

_____

_____

_____

_____

_____

_____

D. Autumn: _____

_____

_____

_____

_____

_____

_____

(Continued)

3. From magazines or catalogs, cut out a picture of an outfit that has good colors for each of the seasonal categories. Mount the pictures in the appropriate boxes.

Winter   **Spring**

Summer   **Autumn**

More Elements of Design

Shape

Activity A

Chapter 11

Name _____

Date _____ Period_____

Find pictures of three currently fashionable outfits with different shapes and mount them in the boxes. Next to each picture, describe the outfit's overall shape and explain how it would flatter or disguise various parts of the human body.

1. _____

_____

_____

_____

_____

_____

_____

_____

_____

_____

_____

_____

_____

_____

_____

_____

_____

_____

_____

_____

(Continued)

2. _____
   _____
   _____
   _____
   _____
   _____
   _____
   _____
   _____
   _____
   _____
   _____
   _____
   _____
   _____
   _____
   _____
   _____
   _____

3. _____
   _____
   _____
   _____
   _____
   _____
   _____
   _____
   _____
   _____
   _____
   _____
   _____
   _____
   _____
   _____
   _____
   _____
   _____
   _____

Creating with Lines

Name _____

Date _____ Period_____

Draw garments on the following two body shapes, highlighting structural and decorative lines that create particular illusions. Next to each figure, describe the illusions you have tried to create.

1. _____

_____

_____

_____

_____

_____

_____

_____

_____

_____

_____

_____

_____

_____

_____

_____

_____

_____

_____

_____

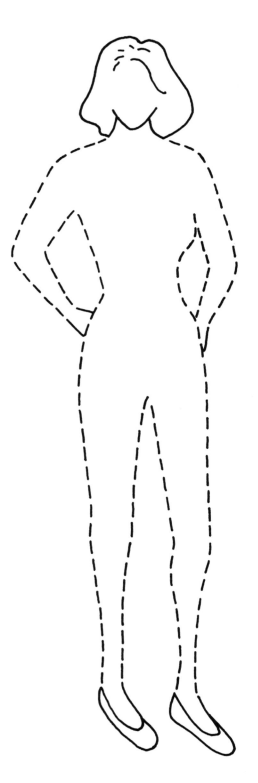

(Continued)

Name _____

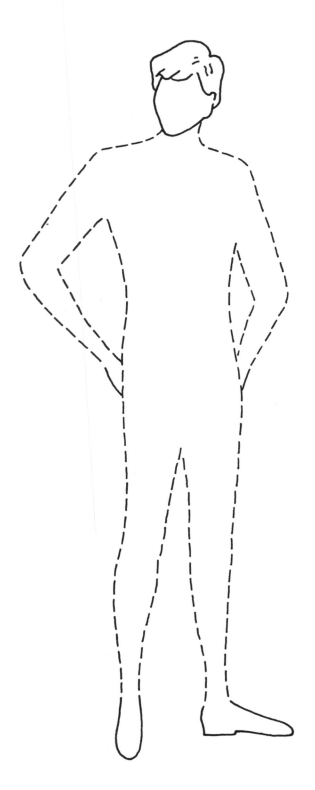

2. _____
_____
_____
_____
_____
_____
_____
_____
_____
_____
_____
_____
_____
_____
_____
_____
_____
_____
_____
_____
_____
_____
_____
_____

Texture

Name _____

Date _____ Period_____

Gather five fabric samples that have various textures and mount them in the boxes. Next to each sample, identify the texture as structural texture or added visual texture. Then describe the texture using words such as bulky, shiny, crisp, bold, subtle, etc. Finally, explain the effects or illusions that could be created by use of the texture in apparel.

1. Type of texture: _____

   Description: _____

   _____

   Effects of the texture in apparel: _____

   _____

   _____

   _____

   _____

   _____

   _____

   _____

   _____

   _____

2. Type of texture: _____

   Description: _____

   _____

   Effects of the texture in apparel: _____

   _____

   _____

   _____

   _____

   _____

   _____

   _____

   _____

   _____

3. Type of texture: _____

   Description: _____

   _____

   Effects of the texture in apparel: _____

   _____

   _____

   _____

   _____

   _____

   _____

   _____

4. Type of texture: _____

   Description: _____

   _____

   Effects of the texture in apparel: _____

   _____

   _____

   _____

   _____

   _____

   _____

   _____

5. Type of texture: _____

   Description: _____

   _____

   Effects of the texture in apparel: _____

   _____

   _____

   _____

   _____

   _____

   _____

Line Categories and Illusions

Activity D   Name _____
Chapter 11   Date _____ Period_____

Place words from the list at the right in each of the general categories on the left.

1. Line Applications

   _____   vertical

   _____   structural

   _____   horizontal

                                              straight

2. Line Directions   decorative

                                              jagged
   _____
                                              diagonal
   _____
                                              curved
   _____

3. Line Types

   _____

   _____

   _____

Explain the illusions created by the following uses of lines in apparel.

4. Vertical lines: _____

   _____

5. Horizontal lines: _____

   _____

6. Lines forming a *T*: _____

   _____

7. Lines forming an *I*: _____

   _____

8. Lines forming a *Y*: _____

   _____

9. Lines spaced far apart: _____

   _____

10. Bold, wide lines: _____

    _____

11. Curved lines: _____

    _____

12. Diagonal lines: _____

    _____

Analyze with Pictures

Name _____

Date _____ Period_____

Look through catalogs and magazines to find a picture of an outfit that you think would improve the way your figure or physique looks. Mount that picture on this page. Then describe how the elements of shape, line, and texture used in that outfit would provide pleasing illusions for your body.

1. Shape: _____

_____

_____

_____

_____

_____

_____

_____

2. Line _____

_____

_____

_____

_____

_____

_____

_____

3. Texture _____

_____

_____

_____

_____

_____

_____

_____

_____

_____

Chapter 12 | Principles of Design

Unscramble the Terms

Activity A

Chapter 12

Name _____

Date _____ Period_____

Unscramble the following words that can be found in Chapter 12 of the textbook. Then write a sentence or two correctly using each word as it relates to the content of the chapter.

1. LECAS: _____

_____

_____

_____

2. AAECLNB: _____

_____

_____

_____

3. STIRNOTIAN: _____

_____

_____

_____

4. IPIPRESCLN FO GIDENS: _____ _____ _____

_____

_____

_____

5. HANROYM: _____

_____

_____

_____

6. RRTOOONPPI: _____

_____

_____

_____

(Continued)

7. ROMLAF CAABLEN: _____ _____

_____

_____

_____

8. SPAMHIES: _____

_____

_____

_____

9. LADARI TEGMARANERN: _____ _____

_____

_____

_____

10. MARFNLIO NABLECA: _____ _____

_____

_____

_____

11. SEDING: _____

_____

_____

_____

12. THRYHM: _____

_____

_____

_____

13. PPIIOONOST: _____

_____

_____

_____

14. GOTANIDAR: _____

_____

_____

_____

15. TENPERHOT: _____

_____

_____

_____

Misfits and More Fits

Name _____

Date _____ Period_____

For each category listed on the left, circle the word or phrase among the rest that does not fit. Then, on the line directly underneath, add one more word or phrase that does fit into that category. Then complete the exercise at the bottom of the page.

1. **Principles of design**

   rhythm   balance   harmony   proportion

   _____

2. **Types of rhythm**

   scale   gradation   opposition   repetition

   _____

3. **To attract attention to areas**

   warm hues   one-color outfits   shiny fabrics   structural accents

   _____

4. **To look taller and thinner**

   one-color outfits   smooth, flat textures   simple, uncluttered look   horizontal emphasis

   _____

5. **To look shorter and wider**

   bulky, heavy textures   subtle prints and plaids   gathers and pleats   light, bright warm colors

   _____

6. **To avoid attention to areas**

   dark, dull colors   plain, unpatterned fabrics   applied decoration   soft fabrics

Respond to the following statements and question.

7. Describe how harmony is achieved. _____

   _____

   _____

8. What is body build? _____

   _____

   _____

9. Describe how personal style is achieved. _____

   _____

   _____

Analyzing "The Latest"

Name _____

Date _____ Period_____

Answer the following questions about the latest fashion trends. Then compare your views with others in the class. Clip pictures from current fashion publications to support your answers.

1. What colors, shapes, lines, and textures are being promoted in current fashions? _____

   _____

   _____

   _____

   _____

   _____

2. What kinds of balance, proportion, emphasis, and rhythm are being used in this season's apparel?

   _____

   _____

   _____

   _____

3. What body build assets are flattered by today's trends? _____

   _____

   _____

   _____

   _____

4. What physical liabilities can be easily camouflaged with the latest trends? _____

   _____

   _____

   _____

   _____

5. What physical liabilities are hard to hide with the latest fashions? _____

   _____

   _____

   _____

   _____

6. Attach a current fashion photo to this page that shows a harmonious outfit. Explain how the elements of design have been used according to the principles of design to create the harmony. _____

   _____

   _____

   _____

   _____

Choose Flattering Outfits

Activity D

Chapter 12

Name _____

Date _____ Period_____

Describe the details of an attractive outfit for each of the following people.

1. Oscar is short and slender, which makes him look younger than his age of 16 years. He wants to look bigger, and seem older, for his job interview at a local fast-food restaurant. _____

   _____

   _____

   _____

   _____

2. Gizelle is 5'2" tall and weighs 145 pounds. She wants to get a new sweater and pair of pants to wear to a party but is unsure about what would make her look taller and more slender. _____

   _____

   _____

   _____

   _____

3. Sue wears size 14 blouses because she has wide shoulders. However, her hips are small, so she fits nicely into size 8 skirts or slacks. She wants to be careful not to look out of proportion._____

   _____

   _____

   _____

   _____

4. Jeff is a star of the basketball team. He is 6'5" tall with a slim build. He gets tired of looking lanky and would like to de-emphasize his "string bean" appearance.

   _____

   _____

   _____

   _____

5. Sometimes Tiffanie's friends comment about her posture, because she has naturally sloping shoulders. Combined with extra long legs, she is often self-conscious about how she thinks she looks. _____

   _____

   _____

   _____

   _____

(Continued)

6. Ann Marie has a straight figure without a defined waistline. She has been wearing casual shirts and jeans. However, now that she is older, she wants to look more like her peers. _____

_____

_____

_____

_____

7. Just like her mother and sisters, Nancy has inherited hips that are large in proportion to the rest of her body. She wants to wear pants like her friends do, but she doesn't want to accentuate what she considers to be a bothersome liability. _____

_____

_____

_____

_____

8. Mark's statuesque frame makes him stand out in a crowd. He has been wearing shirts in large, colorful prints and pants with pleats because they are so comfortable. Some people consider him to be overbearing, even though he is really quite shy. He would like to create a different image. _____

_____

_____

_____

_____

9. Ramone has a good complexion, a nice smile, and attractive eyes, but is bothered by his short, heavy physique. He would like people to notice his assets rather than his liabilities.

_____

_____

_____

_____

10. April has lost several inches from her middle as a result of dieting and working out. She can't afford to buy a new wardrobe but would like to make minor changes to accentuate her slim waistline.

_____

_____

_____

_____

A Personal Style Analysis

Activity E   Name _____

Chapter 12   Date _____ Period_____

Complete the following statements to analyze your own personal style.

My personal height is: tall _____ medium _____ short _____

My body shape is: thin _____ medium _____ heavy _____

My coloring is: eyes _____ hair _____ skin undertone _____

My seasonal color category is: winter _____ spring _____

summer _____ autumn _____

My goal is to look: taller _____ thinner _____ shorter _____ heavier _____

My assets to emphasize are: _____

_____

My liabilities to hide are:_____

_____

Other attributes to note, such as a round face or broad shoulders, include: _____

_____

The best colors for me to wear are: _____

_____

The colors I should avoid are: _____

_____

Shapes I should wear are: _____

_____

Shapes I should avoid are: _____

_____

Lines I should wear are: _____

_____

Lines I should avoid are: _____

_____

Textures I should wear are: _____

_____

Textures I should avoid are: _____

_____

How I might use balance in my apparel includes: _____

_____

(Continued)

Particular design features to use, such as V-necklines, padded shoulders, wide collars, lowered waistlines, etc., include: _____

_____

_____

Considerations for proportion in my clothes are: _____

_____

I could use emphasis to my advantage by: _____

A good type of rhythm in my outfits might be: _____

_____

A synopsis of the "perfect" outfit for my coloring and body shape is: _____

_____

_____

_____

_____

_____

_____

_____

_____

_____

_____

_____

_____

_____

_____

_____

_____

_____

_____

Chapter 13 | The Best Clothes for You

Reactions to Statements

Activity A

Chapter 13

Name _____

Date _____ Period_____

Read the following statements. Then write your reactions to them on the lines provided.

1. Personal attractiveness that results in the best possible image requires some effort. _____

_____

_____

_____

_____

2. People look their best by combining good grooming and clothing sense. _____

_____

_____

_____

_____

3. Lots of teens like to dress like the members of their favorite musical groups. _____

_____

_____

_____

_____

4. People with high clothing consciousness usually achieve higher goals in life than others. _____

_____

_____

_____

_____

5. Colder climates require higher spending costs for clothing. _____

_____

_____

_____

_____

(Continued)

6. Community standards influence the appropriateness of apparel. _____

_____

_____

_____

_____

7. Sometimes it seems that I have lots of clothes but nothing to wear! _____

_____

_____

_____

_____

8. The ideal wardrobe plan would let me dress to forget my clothing. _____

_____

_____

_____

_____

9. The least expensive way to dress is to avoid making wardrobe mistakes. _____

_____

_____

_____

_____

10. My wardrobe should be in a slow state of change. _____

_____

_____

_____

_____

11. My fashion tastes will probably change as I mature. _____

_____

_____

_____

_____

12. When I know I look good, I also feel good. _____

_____

_____

_____

_____

Pictures and Words

Name _____

Date _____ Period_____

Clip pictures from magazines or catalogs to illustrate each of the following statements. Mount the pictures in the boxes. Then explain how each picture illustrates the statement.

1. Apparel should be geared to your lifestyle.

_____

_____

_____

_____

_____

_____

2. Dress for the kind of job you seek.

_____

_____

_____

_____

_____

_____

(Continued)

3. Layered clothing provides an adjustable amount of warmth.

_____

_____

_____

_____

_____

_____

4. Many garments are suitable for a variety of activities.

_____

_____

_____

_____

_____

_____

5. Climate conditions create specific clothing needs.

_____

_____

_____

_____

_____

_____

_____

A Personal Approach to Apparel

Activity C

Chapter 13

Name _____

Date _____ Period_____

Considering that **a well-chosen wardrobe is a collection of**

A. **flattering apparel** (garments and accessories that accentuate assets and play down liabilities) **that keeps you**
B. **suitably dressed** (for your lifestyle, climate, and community standards) at a
C. **reasonable cost** (of time and money),

think about your personal experiences with apparel. Then answer the following questions.

1. How do you feel when you are dressed differently from everyone else at a social event? _____

   _____

   _____

   _____

   _____

2. What is the most treasured item in your wardrobe? Why? _____

   _____

   _____

   _____

   _____

3. What has been your greatest clothing mistake? Why? _____

   _____

   _____

   _____

   _____

4. What do you notice first about the way other people look? _____

   _____

   _____

   _____

   _____

5. What is your most comfortable cold-weather outfit? _____

   _____

   _____

   _____

   _____

(Continued)

6. How do you feel when you wear a new outfit for the first time? Why? _____

_____

_____

_____

_____

7. How do you feel when you get dressed up?_____

_____

_____

_____

_____

8. How do your clothes affect how you act? _____

_____

_____

_____

_____

9. What clothes would you wear if you had an office job? _____

_____

_____

_____

_____

10. What clothes would you wear to a religious service? _____

_____

_____

_____

_____

11. What clothes would you wear for a week of backpacking? _____

_____

_____

_____

_____

12. How are your clothing choices influenced by what others think? _____

_____

_____

_____

_____

The Vocabulary Pyramid

Name _____

Date _____ Period_____

Read the numbered definitions and write the terms in the corresponding spaces on the pyramid.

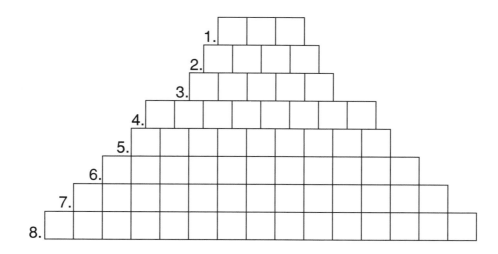

1. A term that represents the passive, timid, delicate elements of personality with small, feminine physical traits.

2. A term that represents the active, rugged elements of personality with large masculine physical traits.

3. A visual representation that serves as the basis for the mental picture of a person or group as seen by others.

4. A person's cleanliness and neatness of nails, hair, teeth, and body.

5. Total pattern of activities that a person does and the places he or she goes.

6. A person's thoughts, feelings, and actions; the total of the characteristics that distinguish a person as an individual.

7. The giving and receiving of verbal and nonverbal messages.

8. A feeling or reaction that people have about someone when they first see or meet him or her. (2 words)

Mixing and Matching

Activity E

Chapter 13

Name _____

Date _____ Period_____

Design a mix-and-match wardrobe by mounting pictures, drawings, and explanations of your ideas on this page. Use about four garments to create as many combinations as possible. Suggest a lifestyle the outfits would be suited for, types of accessories that would be appropriate, and the occasions or places to which the combinations could be worn.

Chapter 14 | Wardrobe Planning

Write the Right Terms

Activity A

Chapter 14

Name _____

Date _____ Period_____

Putting one letter in each blank, write the correct term for each definition below.

1. A(n) __ __ __ __ __ __ __ __ __   __ __ __ __ __ __ __ __ __ __ is an itemized list of all the clothes and accessories a person has.

2. __ __ __ __ __ __ __ __ __ __ __ are articles added to complete or enhance outfits of apparel.

3. Something necessary for a person's continued existence or survival is a(n) __ __ __ __ __.

4. __ __ __ __ __ __ __ __ is stockings, including panty hose, tights, knee highs, and all other socks.

5. __ __ __ __   __ __ __ __ __ __ __ __ is usually made of gold, silver, or platinum and may contain precious or semiprecious stones.

6. __ __ __ __ __ __ __ __ __ __ are cutout decorations that can be used to patch holes in garments or simply to add creative touches.

7. __ __ __ __ __   __ __ __ __ __ __ __ garments are the core of a person's wardrobe and are worn most often.

8. __ __ __ __ __ __ __ __ __ __ are the money, time, and skills a person has available to make wardrobe improvements or carry out other plans.

9. A(n) __ __ __ __ __ __ __ __ __   __ __ __ __ is a "blueprint" of action to update or complete a person's clothes and accessories.

10. A(n) __ __ __ __ __ is a desire for something that gives satisfaction but is not a necessity.

11. __ __ __ __ __ __ __ __ __   __ __ __ __ __ __ __ may be plated with gold or silver, or it may be made of plastic, shells, wood, or unusual materials.

12. __ __ __ __ __ __ __ __ __ __ __ are less expensive garments and accessories that can expand a wardrobe.

13. Items that have top __ __ __ __ __ __ __ __ __ are most important and should be considered first.

14. Having several good quality garments that will last a long time without going out of style is called __.

15. __ __ __ __ __ __ __ __ __ __ __ clothes can be worn during most of the year and include lightweight woolens, knits, and corduroy garments.

16. __ __ __ __ __ __ jewelry is between fine jewelry and costume jewelry in quality and price.

The Final Analysis

Activity B

Chapter 14

Name _____

Date _____ Period_____

Analyze your completed wardrobe inventory chart and your wardrobe planning chart. Then answer the following questions:

1. What did you discover from doing your wardrobe inventory? _____

_____

_____

_____

_____

2. What colors, styles, and specific features are most abundant in the clothing group that you wear a lot?__

_____

_____

_____

_____

3. What action can you take to make specific items that you wear occasionally become clothing you wear a lot?

_____

_____

_____

_____

_____

4. What specific clothing repairs or cleaning must be done, or has been done, to items to allow them to be worn again? _____

_____

_____

_____

_____

5. How can entertainment productions, eye-catching advertising, and attractive store displays cause you to confuse your clothing wants with your needs? _____

_____

_____

_____

_____

6. How will you now go about carrying out your wardrobe plan? _____

_____

_____

_____

Personal Reactions

Name _____

Date _____ Period_____

Read the following statements and indicate your reaction to each. Check if you think the statement is an interesting aspect of wardrobe coordination, if it seems uninteresting to you, or if you are unsure about your feelings toward it. You will not be graded on your responses. Then choose what you feel the most interesting statement of the group is and explain your reaction to it in detail.

Interesting	Uninteresting	Unsure
_____	_____	_____
_____	_____	_____
_____	_____	_____
_____	_____	_____
_____	_____	_____
_____	_____	_____
_____	_____	_____
_____	_____	_____

1. People's "clothing standards" are their ideas about the quality and quantity of clothing considered essential in their wardrobes. It is also the length of time they consider garments to be wearable before discarding them.

2. Suspenders are an accessory that first appeared around 1700 in Europe but didn't become widely used until about 1780. They were and still are called "braces" in England. Today they are sometimes worn for personal expression.

3. Commercial pattern companies help home sewers build coordinating wardrobes. In one envelope, they may offer patterns for several mix-and-match garments.

4. "Fashion Accessory Expo" is a quarterly trade fair in New York City where more than 600 accessory designers display jewelry, scarves, handbags, and other items.

5. Many people who choose not to make their clothes still want to have at least enough sewing skills to do simple repairs and alterations. They also believe that a basic knowledge of sewing helps them judge the quality of merchandise when they shop for clothes.

6. Cloisonné jewelry, developed in Asia, has deeply colored and polished enamel designs outlined with set-in copper lines.

7. A study of today's young, image-conscious professionals has shown that they consider comfort almost as important as a professional look. This seems logical, since tugging at uncomfortable garments does not contribute to a chic, well-dressed appearance!

8. The recent popularity of cotton sweaters that are worn year-round has extended people's clothing budgets and allowed them to comfortably layer clothes for different climate conditions. A cotton sweater is a multipurpose, seasonless garment.

Interesting	Uninteresting	Unsure
_____	_____	_____
_____	_____	_____
_____	_____	_____
_____	_____	_____
_____	_____	_____
_____	_____	_____

9. Costume jewelry is also called "fashion jewelry." Often costume jewelry fads create inexpensive fashion.
10. Corporate "casual days" allow people to save money because the same clothes can be worn to work and to casual social events.
11. "Cross-shopping" is the recent consumer trend of combining purchases from both ends of the price sale. You might plan to buy an inexpensive skirt from a discount store to wear with a luxurious silk blouse from an upscale shop.
12. The simpler a garment design is, the easier it is to alter its fit or update it to a fashionable look.
13. Wardrobe planning is like gardening—you have to continually weed and plant parts of it!
14. More consumers are now sticking with their individual style in apparel choices rather than succumbing to fads.

The most interesting statement is #_____ because _____

_____

_____

_____

_____

_____

_____

_____

_____

_____

_____

_____

_____

_____

_____

_____

Accessory Show and Tell

Activity D

Chapter 14

Name _____

Date _____ Period_____

Cut out and mount pictures of specific accessories from 6 of the 11 different categories listed in the textbook.
For each one, tell how it might be used and/or what types of events might be appropriate for its wear.

Category: _____

Uses: _____

_____

_____

_____

Category: _____

Uses: _____

_____

_____

_____

(Continued)

Category: _____

Uses: _____

_____

_____

_____

Category: _____

Uses: _____

_____

_____

_____

Category: _____

Uses: _____

_____

_____

_____

Category: _____

Uses: _____

_____

_____

_____

Record Your Resources

Name _____

Date _____ Period _____

Complete the following chart by describing your resources and expenses during a typical week. Then, after analyzing the information, explain how you could maximize your resources to achieve your wardrobe plan and other objectives you may have.

	Category	Description
R E S O U R C E S	**Time** (how much free time available and when)	
	Money (allowance, gifts, wages, etc.)	
	Skills (abilities and talents)	
E X P E N S E S	**Fixed expenses** (transportation, daily lunches, etc.)	
	Variable or occasional expenses (movie, dinner out, etc.)	

(Continued)

Name _____

To maximize my resources, I could _____

_____
_____
_____
_____
_____
_____
_____
_____
_____
_____
_____
_____
_____
_____
_____
_____
_____
_____
_____
_____
_____
_____
_____
_____
_____
_____
_____
_____
_____
_____
_____
_____
_____
_____
_____
_____

Chapter 15

Being a Smart Shopper

Rating Retailers

Activity A

Chapter 15

Name _____

Date _____ Period_____

Describe one of the apparel items you plan to buy soon. _____

Then do actual shopping research to answer the following questions.

1. Name five retailers (include specific stores, mail-order catalogs, Internet sites, etc.) where this type of item is available. _____

_____

_____

2. Which retailers seem to have the highest quality of this item?_____

_____

_____

3. Which retailers have the lowest prices for the item?_____

_____

_____

4. Which retailers offer the best choices of styles, colors, and sizes for this item? _____

_____

_____

5. Where do you feel the most comfortable with the retail atmosphere, employees, and services? _____

_____

_____

6. Which retailers have good locations for you? _____

_____

_____

7. Which retailers are open during the times you want to shop? _____

_____

_____

8. Did you pick any of the retailers because of their advertising? If so, which ones?_____

_____

_____

(Continued)

9. Did you pick any of the retailers because of your feelings of loyalty to shop there? If so, which ones?

   _____

   _____

10. From which of these retailers have you or your close friends or relatives made satisfactory purchases of similar items in the past? _____

    _____

    Unsatisfactory purchases? _____

    _____

11. After analyzing your answers to the above questions, from which retailer would you purchase the item? Why? _____

    _____

    _____

    _____

    _____

    _____

    _____

    _____

    _____

    _____

12. Does the retailer offer return and refund privileges, exchanges, and rain checks for specials that have been sold out? _____

    _____

13. Does the retailer offer services you want, such as the use of credit cards, check cashing, and gift wrapping?

    _____

    _____

14. What types of products would you probably not purchase from this retailer? _____

    _____

    _____

15. Describe the value of periodically doing this type of analysis, especially before making a major purchase.

    _____

    _____

    _____

    _____

    _____

    _____

Preparing Ahead

Activity B

Chapter 15

Name _____

Date _____ Period_____

After identifying your wardrobe needs from Chapter 14, prepare ahead for your purchases by responding to the following directions:

1. **Make a list**
   Make a list of your clothing and accessory needs, focusing on your priority needs. Be specific about styles, colors, and cost estimates.

   _____

   _____

   _____

   _____

   _____

2. **Gather information**
   A. Cut out a fashion article from a newspaper or magazine and mount it in the box. Tell what helpful information it includes.

(Continued)

B. Browse at a nearby department store or mall. Write down what information you discovered.

_____
_____
_____
_____
_____
_____
_____

C. If you have mail-order catalogs and/or access to a computer, look for your needed items and write down what information you discovered.

_____
_____
_____
_____
_____
_____
_____
_____

3. **Evaluate advertising**

Clip a clothing advertisement that appeals to you and mount it here. Write an analysis of the useful information provided. How does the ad try to persuade you to buy the item?

_____
_____
_____
_____
_____
_____
_____
_____
_____
_____
_____
_____
_____
_____
_____
_____
_____
_____
_____

Laws That Relate to Consumers

Activity C   Name _____

Chapter 15   Date _____ Period_____

Complete the following exercises.

1. Name and describe the five government regulations that apply to apparel and are discussed in Chapter 15 of the textbook.

A. _____
   _____
   _____
   _____
   _____

B. _____
   _____
   _____
   _____
   _____
   _____

C. _____
   _____
   _____
   _____
   _____
   _____

D. _____
   _____
   _____
   _____
   _____

E. _____
   _____
   _____
   _____
   _____

(Continued)

2. Read the following statements. Place a check in the column that best represents how you feel about each. Then analyze your score according to the directions.

STATEMENTS	ALMOST ALWAYS	SOMETIMES	ALMOST NEVER
a. Consumers need government protection.			
b. Consumer laws are designed to protect consumers.			
c. Although people's needs vary, consumer laws are aimed at meeting the needs of the majority.			
d. Consumers have the right and responsibility to inform legislators of their opinions.			
e. Consumers should expect businesses to be serious about consumers' rights.			
f. Consumers should take their responsibilities just as seriously as their rights.			
g. Consumer laws are worth the added costs they pass along to consumers.			
h. Consumer laws help to assure consumer safety.			
i. Consumer laws help to inform consumers.			
j. Consumer laws help consumers make wise choices.			

Analysis

If most of your check marks are in the "Almost Always" column, you show a positive attitude toward the effect of consumer laws on consumers.

If most of your check marks are in the "Almost Never" column, you show a negative attitude toward the effect of consumer laws on consumers.

If most of your check marks are in the "Sometimes" column or scattered across the chart, you are undecided about the value of consumer laws.

What is your attitude toward consumer laws?

_____

_____

_____

_____

_____

_____

_____

_____

_____

Consumer Complaints

Activity D   Name _____

Chapter 15   Date _____ Period_____

Describe a consumer problem that you or someone you know has had with a garment purchased recently.

1. Item description: _____

   _____

2. Complaint:_____

   _____

   _____

   _____

3. What action was taken? _____

   _____

   _____

   _____

4. How was the problem handled?_____

   _____

   _____

   _____

5. Why should you complain if a product or service is not satisfactory? _____

   _____

   _____

   _____

6. Write a sample complaint letter about the problem and attach it to this page.

Smart Shopper Crossword

Name _____

Date _____ Period_____

Complete the crossword puzzle using the clues listed:

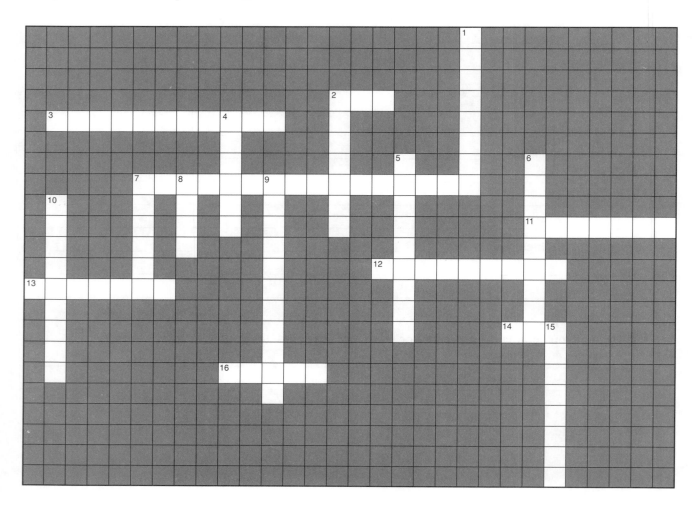

(Continued)

Across:

2. The _____ Products Labeling Act specifies that information required on labels and in advertising of garments of/or containing fur.

3. Stores use _____ to catch consumers' interest in merchandise.

7. All shoppers have consumer _____ that include acting in appropriate ways.

11. Good shopping _____ include being courteous and polite, waiting your turn, and stating your needs clearly to salespeople.

12. _____ is the covering, wrapper, or container in which merchandise is often placed.

13. _____ buying is sudden and not carefully thought-out purchasing.

14. The initials for the government agency that enforces garment labeling laws are _____.

16. A _____-conscious person is aware of the cost of merchandise and his or her personal financial resources.

Down:

1. _____ are detachable "signs" affixed to the out side of garments, containing promotional information.

2. The state of being aware of and wanting new items, usually to gain the approval of others, is known as being _____ conscious.

4. The purpose of advertising is to sell and to _____.

5. _____ are the criteria set by authorities who judge products to verify levels of quality.

6. The _____ Care Labeling Rule requires manufacturers to attach clear and complete care labels to apparel items.

7. Consumers have _____, and they should be able to have certain expectations from the goods and services they buy.

8. Salespeople may not give reliable advice to shoppers because their job is to _____ merchandise.

9. _____ is the stealing of merchandise from a store.

10. The _____ Fabrics Act specifies burning stan dards of fabrics in clothing and many household textiles.

15. One of the branches of the Federal Trade Commission is the Bureau of _____ Protections.

Shopping Manners

Activity F

Chapter 15

Name _____

Date _____ Period_____

Visit a department store or apparel store. Observe customers and salespeople for 20 to 30 minutes. Watch for examples of good and bad shopping manners from the customers, and strong and weak performance from the salespeople. Write a brief description of your observations here and discuss them with others in class.

Examples of good shopping manners: _____

_____

_____

_____

_____

_____

_____

Examples of bad shopping manners:_____

_____

_____

_____

_____

_____

_____

Examples of strong salesperson performance: _____

_____

_____

_____

_____

_____

_____

Examples of weak salesperson performance: _____

_____

_____

_____

_____

_____

_____

Making the Right Purchase

Ring Around the Letter

Activity A

Name _____

Chapter 16

Date _____ Period_____

Complete the following statements about smart purchasing. Then arrange the circled letters to spell a phrase relating to the content of the textbook. Use the phrase in the sentence at the end of this activity.

1. A(n) __ __ __◯__ __ __ __ __ __ __   __ __ __ __ is a credit arrangement with a down payment toward a purchase and a contract that specifies the periodic payments and finance charges.

2. When a checking account is ◯__ __ __ __ __ __ __ __, it has checks written against it for more money that it contains.

3. Comparing the qualities and prices of same or similar items in different stores before buying is called __ __◯__ __ __ __ __ __   __ __ __ __ __ __ __ __.

4. The level of performance, or __ __◯__ __ __ __, of a product is often described as low, medium, or high.

5. A(n) __ __ __ __ __ __ __ __ __◯is a distinctive symbol or name that identifies the goods of a particular seller or manufacturer.

6. A(n) __ __◯__ __ __   __ __ __ __ __ is usually made of plastic and establishes the holder's ability to charge goods and services at participating businesses.

7. Your __ __ __ __ __◯__   __ __ __ __ __ __ __ is an evaluation of your financial standing based on past records of debt repayment, financial status, etc.

8. When a(n) __ __ __◯purchase is made, the full cost of what is bought is paid with money, check, or debit card.

9. Writing a(n) __ __◯__ __ to make a purchase gives you another record of your spending, since when it is canceled, it is a good receipt.

10. A(n) __ __ __ __ __ __   __ __◯__ deducts money from a person's bank account and deposits it in a store's account when a purchase is made.

11. A(n) __ __ __ __ __ __ __ __   __ __◯__ is a paper signed when a credit purchase is made that tells what, when, where, and for what price the transaction took place.

12. A(n) __ __ __◯__ __ __ is a favorable purchase; a high value of merchandise in exchange for a small amount of money.

13. The __ __ __ __ __◯-__ __ -__ __ __ __ __ __ __ __ Law requires grantors of consumer credit to reveal the true cost of credit in uniform, easy-to-understand terms.

(Continued)

14. _ _ _ _ _ _ ◯_ _ _ _ _ _ _ _ combines two or more specific garment sizes into general categories such as small, medium, and large.

15. Making purchases that are sudden and not carefully thought out is called _ _◯_ _ _ _ _ _ _ _ _ _ _.

16. An item's _ _ _◯_ is its degree of worth or benefit.

17. _ _ _◯_ _ _ _ _ _ _ is the room a person needs to move comfortably in a garment.

18. Your ◯_ _ _ _ _ _ _ _ _ _ is the maximum financial amount that you may have outstanding on a charge or other credit account.

19. A(n) _◯_ _ _ _ - _ _ _ charge account must be paid in full by a certain day of every month.

20. In a(n) _◯_ _ _ _ _ purchase, you select an item and pay for it through an initial deposit and additional payments. When you have paid the full price, you receive the item.

21. A(n) _ _◯_ _ _ _ _ is money borrowed from a bank, credit union, or finance company that is repaid with interest according to a written agreement.

22. A(n) _◯_ _ _ _ _ _ _ _ _ _ _ _ _ account can be paid in full or in monthly installments with finance charges.

Circled letters: _
                 1 2 3 4 5 6 7 8 9 10 11 12 13 14 15 16 17 18 19 20 21 22

In this chapter, we studied how _____ _____ _____ _____ _____,

which is illustrated by this sentence: _____

_____

_____

_____

Comparison Shopping

Activity B

Chapter 16

Name _____

Date _____ Period_____

Select a type of garment you might be interested in buying, such as a shirt, sweater, or coat. Then shop in a department store or apparel stores to compare the prices and points of quality of three garments with different brand names. Using the chart below, rate each garment. Then add the numbers in the columns for a total comparison.

Type of garment: _____

Garment A: Brand _____

              Price _____

Garment B: Brand _____

              Price _____

Garment C: Brand _____

              Price _____

Ratings:

Excellent 4

Good... 3

Fair.. 2

Poor 1

Not applicable ....NA

Garment	A	B	C
1. It has an attached label that tells fiber content, country of orgin, care instructions, and identification of producer.			
2. The care requirements are to my liking.			
3. The fabric is even, flawless, and suitable for the garment and my needs.			
4. The seams are smooth, strong, and finished neatly.			
5. The stitching is straight, even, and neat.			
6. Hems are even, secure, not noticeable, and of proper width for the garment.			
7. Reinforcements are included at points of strain.			
8. Fasteners are suitable, functional, and attractive.			
9. Pockets, collars, cuffs, and waistbands are well constructed.			
10. The garment is durable for long wear.			
11. The design will probably be in style for a long time.			
12. The fit is correct and becoming.			
13. The price is reasonable for the item.			
14. The color is right for me and for my wardrobe coordination.			
15. The manufacturer has a good name and reputation.			
Totals			

(Continued)

16. Which garment would you buy after doing the comparison shopping? Why?

_____
_____
_____
_____
_____
_____
_____
_____
_____
_____
_____
_____
_____
_____
_____
_____
_____
_____

17. Why is it important to comparison shop for major purchases?

_____
_____
_____
_____
_____
_____
_____
_____
_____
_____
_____
_____
_____
_____
_____
_____

Assemble the Words

Name _____

Date _____ Period_____

Combine letters from the three jumbled columns to form terms relating to each heading. Then use each term in a sentence relating to the subject matter of the textbook.

Specific points of quality for judging value:

1. _____ =   fas   imm   ets

2. _____ =   tr   ni   hing

3. _____ =   st   ten   ngs

4. _____ =   li   ck   ings

5. _____ =   po   itc   ers

Sentences:

1. _____
   _____
   _____
   _____

2. _____
   _____
   _____
   _____
   _____

3. _____
   _____
   _____
   _____
   _____

4. _____
   _____
   _____
   _____

5. _____
   _____
   _____
   _____

(Continued)

Name _____

Size range categories:

6. _____ = wo   ni   n's
7. _____ = m   me   s
8. _____ = ju   ss   or
9. _____ = mi   en   es

Sentences:

6. _____
_____
_____
_____

7. _____
_____
_____
_____

8. _____
_____
_____
_____

9. _____
_____
_____
_____

Types of sales:

10. _____ = inv   krup   white
11. _____ = Jan   ir   ory
12. _____ = f   eara   tcy
13. _____ = ban   ent   e
14. _____ = cle   uary   nce

Sentences:

10. _____
_____
_____

11. _____
_____
_____
_____

(Continued)

12. _____

_____

_____

_____

13. _____

_____

_____

_____

14. _____

_____

_____

_____

Ways to pay:

15. _____ = cr   ec   ment

16. _____ = ch   ed   h

17. _____ = ins   as   k

18. _____ = c   tall   it

Sentences:

15. _____

_____

_____

_____

_____

16. _____

_____

_____

_____

_____

17. _____

_____

_____

_____

_____

18. _____

_____

_____

_____

_____

Smart Consumer Maze

Name _____

Date _____ Period_____

Draw a line through this maze from "start" to "smart purchase." As you do this, your line should cross 12 terms that apply to being a smart consumer. When you have finished the maze, write the 12 terms in the order they appear in the maze to create a list that reviews smart consumer purchasing procedures. Then make a list of the unwise consumer practices that your line did not cross.

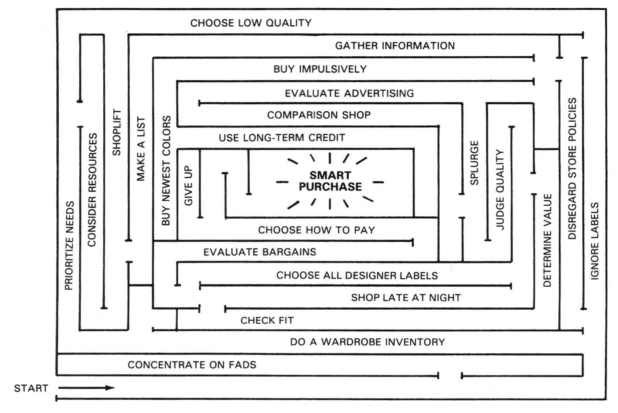

Smart Consumer Procedures	Unwise Consumer Practices
1. _____	_____
2. _____	_____
3. _____	_____
4. _____	_____
5. _____	_____
6. _____	_____
7. _____	_____
8. _____	_____
9. _____	_____
10. _____	_____
11. _____	_____
12. _____	_____

Purchasing Habits

Name _____

Date _____ Period_____

Determine whether the purchasing habits described here are good or bad. Write "good" or "bad" in the short space in each answer. Then continue with an explanation of your opinion.

1. Before shopping, Liam outlines on paper what he already has and what he needs to update his wardrobe. This is a _____ habit because _____

   _____

   _____

   _____

2. Kevin uses just a few basic colors in his wardrobe so he can mix and match everything. This is a _____ habit because_____

   _____

   _____

   _____

3. Wendy buys something every time she goes to the mall whether she needs it or not. This is a _____ habit because _____

   _____

   _____

4. Francesca does comparison shopping, especially for expensive basic items. This is a _____ habit because _____

   _____

   _____

   _____

5. Kassandra always tries on garments before purchasing them to make sure they fit. This is a _____ habit because _____

   _____

   _____

6. Nate uses his sewing skills to make simple garments and to repair and update old items. He spends most of his clothing money on items like jackets, sweaters, and shoes. This is a _____ habit because

   _____

   _____

7. Doug buys clothes without considering the care they will require. This is a _____ habit because

   _____

   _____

(Continued)

8. Carlos checks for quality of construction before deciding if a purchase is a good value for the price. This
   is a _____ habit because_____
   _____
   _____

9. Anne has found a brand of jeans that fit her well. She plans to buy this brand again. This is a _____ habit
   because_____
   _____
   _____

10. Yolanda almost always buys clothes on impulse. This is a _____ habit because_____
    _____
    _____

11. When Ben shops for merchandise on the Internet, he checks specifics about items through the Internet—
    www.fashionmall.com and Web sites of several individual retailers. This is a _____ habit because_____
    _____
    _____

12. List some of your buying habits here. Analyze which ones are good. Then explain which ones should be
    changed and how. _____
    _____
    _____
    _____
    _____
    _____
    _____
    _____
    _____
    _____
    _____
    _____
    _____
    _____
    _____
    _____

Chapter 17 | Apparel for People with Special Needs

Special Needs Match-Up

Activity A

Chapter 17

Name _____

Date _____ Period _____

Match the following definitions with the terms by placing the correct letter next to each number.

_____ 1. The assembled minimal needs of clothing and textile goods for a newborn infant.

_____ 2. These are 100 percent cotton and usually have a "hood" across one corner to put over a baby's head for warmth after the bath.

_____ 3. Attributes of garments that let children, as well as people with disabilities and older people, dress themselves.

_____ 4. Heavy-duty types of snaps.

_____ 5. Cloth or vinyl coverings tied at the back of the neck and used to protect the clothes, especially for infants and young children.

_____ 6. Apparel for pregnant women.

_____ 7. Attributes for garments that allow them to be "expanded" as children grow.

_____ 8. Layette items, usually made of vinyl, that are used over cloth diapers.

_____ 9. A young child, usually between 1 and 2 1/2 years of age, who is actively moving or walking.

_____ 10. A young child between the ages of 2 1/2 and 5 years.

_____ 11. A full-length infant garment with sleeves and a drawstring closing at the bottom.

_____ 12. A full-length infant garment with sleeves that is closed in the front or back with snaps or ties.

_____ 13. All the apparel a person takes on a trip.

_____ 14. Attributes of garments that reduce the chances of injury or other hazardous occurrences.

_____ 15. Basic infant garment of folded cloth or other absorbent material drawn up between the legs and fastened near the waist.

_____ 16. A person who has a physical or mental disability that limits his or her activities.

_____ 17. The length of the body from shoulder to crotch.

_____ 18. Infant "coveralls" with enclosed feet made of two-way stretch fabrics.

A. back rise

B. bibs

C. buttons

D. comfort features

E. diaper

F. gown (infant)

G. grippers

H. growth features

I. disabled

J. hand-me-downs

K. hoods

L. infant

M. kimono (infant)

N. layette

O. maternity fashions

P. preschooler

Q. safety features

R. self-help features

S. self-independence

T. stretch suits

U. toddler

V. towels (infant)

W. travel wardrobe

X. trunk measurement

Y. waist measurement

Z. waterproof pants

Note the Similarities

Name _____

Date _____ Period_____

Make lists of desired characteristics of apparel for infants, children, older people, and people with disabilities. Then discuss why many of the characteristics appear in all or several of the lists.

1. **Desired characteristics for infant apparel**

_____

_____

_____

_____

_____

_____

_____

_____

_____

_____

_____

2. **Desired characteristics for children's apparel**

_____

_____

_____

_____

_____

_____

_____

_____

_____

_____

_____

3. **Desired characteristics of apparel for older people**

_____

_____

_____

_____

_____

_____

_____

_____

_____

_____

4. **Desired characteristics of apparel for people with disabilities**

_____

_____

_____

_____

_____

_____

_____

_____

_____

_____

A Special Needs Apparel Interview

Activity C

Chapter 17

Name _____

Date _____ Period_____

For a mock television talk show, write out six pertinent questions you would ask a fashion designer or apparel manufacturing executive of infant or young children's clothing. Then assume the identity of the person being interviewed. Think about what factors you consider to be important in bringing out a line of clothes for the coming season. Then have a classmate ask you the questions in front of the class for an exclusive interview!

1. _____
_____
_____
_____
_____

2. _____
_____
_____
_____
_____

3. _____
_____
_____
_____
_____

4. _____
_____
_____
_____
_____

5. _____
_____
_____
_____
_____

6. _____
_____
_____
_____
_____

Test Questions to Ask

Activity D

Chapter 17

Name _____

Date _____ Period_____

Prepare two test questions and answers for each of the following chapter headings. Write your correct answers on another piece of paper. Then exchange papers with a classmate to answer each other's questions.

Apparel Needs of Infants.

1. _____
   _____
   _____

2. _____
   _____
   _____

Clothing for Young Children.

3. _____
   _____
   _____

4. _____
   _____
   _____

Clothing for Older People.

5. _____
   _____
   _____

6. _____
   _____
   _____

Apparel for People with Disabilities.

7. _____
   _____
   _____

8. _____
   _____
   _____

Travel Wardrobes.

9. _____
   _____
   _____

10. _____
    _____

Express Your Thoughts

Name _____

Date _____ Period_____

Think about the following statements and write your reaction to each on the lines provided.

1. Baby outfits are so cute that sometimes people buy lots of them, even though the garments may be worn only a few times before the baby outgrows them. _____

   _____

   _____

   _____

   _____

2. Even though disposable diapers are expensive, wasteful of natural resources, and the source of a great deal of garbage, many people use them on infants because they are so comfortable and convenient. _____

   _____

   _____

   _____

   _____

3. Infant apparel sizes are listed either by age in months or by descriptive terms such as small, medium, and large. However, just as for other apparel, sizing systems may vary from manufacturer to manufacturer.

   _____

   _____

   _____

   _____

4. Garments for young children often have self-help features that enable children to dress independently.

   _____

   _____

   _____

   _____

5. From childhood to old age, it is important to have clothes that help to promote social acceptance and self-esteem. _____

   _____

   _____

   _____

   _____

(Continued)

6. Hand-me-downs and sewing some items of young children's apparel can save quite a bit of money. ____

_____

_____

_____

_____

7. As people age, their body proportions may change so much that they can no longer wear standard-sized, ready-to-wear clothing. _____

_____

_____

_____

_____

8. Apparel that is comfortable, functional, and attractive can enhance the productivity and independence of people with disabilities. _____

_____

_____

_____

_____

9. Sewing machines are now available with special features that help blind people and people with disabilities sew. _____

_____

_____

_____

_____

10. Increasing numbers of women in the workforce have created a greater demand for maternity fashions with a professional look._____

_____

_____

_____

_____

11. A good travel wardrobe consists of a few coordinated garments that are lightweight and wrinkle-resistant.

_____

_____

_____

_____

12. Since luggage is sometimes lost or damaged during air travel, more people are using only carry-on luggage that has less space to pack clothes. _____

_____

_____

_____

My Care of Clothes

Activity A   Name _____

Chapter 18   Date _____ Period_____

Read the following statements. Place a check in the column that best represents how you feel about each. Then analyze your score according to the directions that are given. (You will not be graded on your ratings.)

STATEMENTS	ALMOST ALWAYS	SOMETIMES	ALMOST NEVER
1. I put on old clothes to do tough, dirty jobs.			
2. After wearing garments, I either put them with the dirty clothes or put them away neatly.			
3. If garments need dry cleaning or repairs, I put them where they will get the proper treatment.			
4. I empty the pockets of garments before hanging them up.			
5. I repair and mend apparel items before I launder or clean them.			
6. I read and follow the directions on the permanent care labels in my clothes.			
7. I keep my closets, shelves, and drawers clean, neat, and well-organized.			
8. I store items together that are used together or that are similar.			
9. I store items so they are easy to find at a glance.			
10. I fold, rather than hang, knitted garments.			
11. I carefully put away clothing that will not be used until the next season.			
12. I wash or clean dirty apparel before storing it for a future season.			
13. I give prompt attention to spots and stains on apparel.			
14. Before using a cleaning product, I read the manufacturer's directions and warnings.			
15. I know what stain removal methods to use for particular stains on various fabrics.			

(Continued)

Analysis

If most of your check marks are in the "Almost Always" column, you show a positive attitude toward the care of your clothes.

If most of your check marks are in the "Almost Never" column, you don't show much concern toward the care of your clothes.

If most of your check marks are in the "Sometimes" column or scattered across the chart, you are inconsistent about, or undecided about, the value of caring for your clothes properly.

What is your attitude toward the care of your clothes? _____

_____

_____

_____

_____

Why do you think you have that attitude toward the care of your clothes? _____

_____

_____

_____

_____

_____

_____

After reviewing your check marks on the chart, what changes do you feel you should make to properly care

for your clothes? _____

_____

_____

_____

_____

_____

_____

_____

_____

Note the Differences

Name _____

Date _____ Period _____

What is the difference between:

1. Soaking and sponging? _____

   _____

   _____

   _____

   _____

2. Lint-attracting fabrics and lint-producing fabrics? _____

   _____

   _____

   _____

   _____

3. Detergents and soaps? _____

   _____

   _____

   _____

   _____

4. Surfactants and builders? _____

   _____

   _____

   _____

   _____

5. Enzymes and sizings? _____

   _____

   _____

   _____

   _____

6. Chlorine bleach and oxygen bleach? _____

   _____

   _____

   _____

   _____

   _____

(Continued)

7. Fabric softeners and water softeners? _____

_____

_____

_____

_____

8. Line drying and flat drying? _____

_____

_____

_____

_____

9. Ironing and pressing? _____

_____

_____

_____

_____

10. Ironing board and sleeve board? _____

_____

_____

_____

_____

11. Pressing cloth and pressing mitt? _____

_____

_____

_____

_____

12. Professional dry cleaning and coin-operated dry cleaning? _____

_____

_____

_____

_____

Laundry Product Comparisons

Activity C

Chapter 18

Name _____

Date _____ Period_____

At a supermarket, compare the information on the packages of four same-type laundry products. Use the information to complete this chart. Then answer the questions on the lines provided.

	Product 1	Product 2	Product 3	Product 4
Brand name				
Name of manufacturer				
Net contents and price				
Performance claims				
Directions for use				
Special precautions				
Other helpful information				
Probable effectiveness				

(Continued)

Name _____

1. Which product in the chart do you think would be the best? _____

   Why? _____

   _____

   _____

2. Rank the top five reasons you might choose a laundry product by putting the numbers 1 through 5 next
   to your choices from this list.

   _____ size of package   _____ price

   _____ special discount or coupon   _____ safety of product use

   _____ convenience of use   _____ advertising

   _____ manufacturer's reputation   _____ package appearance

   _____ type (powder, liquid, etc.)   _____ color or fragrance

   _____ a friend or relative's advice   _____ familiarity of brand name

   _____ its environmental safety   _____ a free sample was sent

   _____ my own experience with it   _____ label information

3. Put a check next to the phrase in each column that describes you as a buyer of laundry products.

   _____ very interested   _____ quite well-informed

   _____ somewhat interested   _____ as well informed as most

   _____ not interested at all   _____ not very well-informed

4. Consider the laundry products you and your family use. Are any of them especially wonderful or
   disappointing? Explain. _____

   _____

   _____

   _____

   _____

5. Describe a laundry product and create an advertising theme or slogan for it. _____

   _____

   _____

   _____

   _____

   _____

   _____

Storage Ideas

Name _____

Date _____ Period _____

1. List the categories of items you keep in your closet. _____

_____

_____

_____

_____

2. Describe how all the items fit in your closet. _____

_____

_____

_____

_____

3. Draw a diagram here showing how you could make better use of the space in your closet. Indicate where the various categories of items would be stored.

SHELF

BAR

FLOOR

Clothing Care and Laundering Selection

Activity E

Chapter 18

Name _____

Date _____ Period _____

Complete the crossword puzzle using the clues listed. Then complete the multiple choice activity that follows.

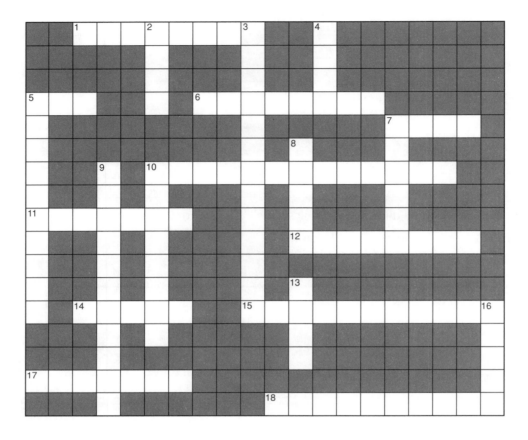

Across:

1. The bunch of clothes put into a laundry machine to be washed together at one time.
5. _____-sudsing detergents contain suds control agents and are recommended for "suds sensitive" washers.
6. Ingredients in laundry products that inactivate hard water minerals.
7. _____ drying of laundered garments is usually used for wool, knit, and leather items.
10. The ability to be broken down into natural waste products that do not harm the environment.
11. Proteins that speed up chemical reactions. In laundry products, they help break down certain soils and stains into simpler forms that can be removed easier.
12. Sizings that restore body and crispness to fabrics that have become limp from laundering and wear.

14. Laundry products that neutralize the mineral ions found in hard water, or hold them in solution, are _____ softeners.
15. Agents in detergents that reduce the surface tension of water, help loosen and remove soil, and suspend the soil in the water until it is drained.
17. The process of applying heat and pressure with a gliding motion to remove wrinkles from damp, washable fabrics.
18. Granular or liquid laundry products made synthetically from chemicals that suspend and hold dirt away from clothes during washing.

Down:

2. _____-sudsing detergents are considered to be all-purpose.
3. Sanitizers that are sometimes used in laundering to control or eliminate infections by reducing or killing microorganisms.
4. _____ drying is done by hanging clothes on a clothesline, usually outside. *(Continued)*

5. The process of washing apparel or other textile items with water and laundry products.

7. Laundry products that control static electricity and give softness and fluffiness to washable fabrics are _____ softeners.

8. A process to remove wrinkles from fabric by placing an iron on the fabric and then lifting it without sliding the iron across the fabric.

9. The process of cleaning textile items with non-water liquid solvents or absorbent compounds. (2 words)

10. Chlorine or oxygen-type laundry products used to clean, whiten, and brighten clothes.

13. _____-drying is done by hanging wet items on a nonrusting hanger or rack without squeezing or wringing.

16. Biodegradable bar or granule cleaning products made mostly from natural fats and lye.

Select the best way to care for each item described and write the letter in the blank.

_____1. Your new navy T-shirt sneaked into the washing machine and turned your white, 100 percent cotton blouse light blue.
A. Soak blouse in saltwater and throw away T-shirt.
B. Dye blouse darker blue and hand wash T-shirt in the future.
C. Bleach blouse now and sort laundry in the future.
D. Take both items to a dry cleaner.

_____2. Your wool burgundy sweater that Grandma knit is dirty from several wearings but has no care label.
A. Hand wash in cold water and hang on padded hanger to air dry.
B. Hand wash in cold water, roll in towel, and block to original shape.
C. Machine wash in cold water and iron to restore new look.
D. Hand wash in warm water and fluff-dry in dryer.

_____3. Your dark green polyester/cotton corduroy slacks have a bloodstain from the dog's cut paw.
A. Rinse immediately in cool water with enzyme presoak, rub with detergent, an launder.
B. Rub with ice, scrape blood with dull knife, and launder.
C. Wash with chlorine bleach and dry as usual.
D. Rinse immediately in warm chlorine bleach solution, rub with detergent, and launder.

_____4. Mustard oozed out of the end of your hot dog and slopped onto your favorite blue jeans.
A. Wash as soon as possible in hot water with chlorine bleach.
B. Spray with prewash or rub with soap, soak with detergent, and launder with oxygen bleach.
C. Rub with rounded back of silver spoon, soak in alkaline solution, and launder as usual.
D. Soak in salt water, rub with baking soda paste, and launder in cold water with warm rinse.

_____5. Your tan shorts have a large grass stain, and tomorrow is "tan shorts day" at school.
A. This stain does not come out; sew a fun, colorful patch over the stain.
B. Soak in strong detergent and hot water.
C. Use an enzyme presoak, rub with detergent, and launder.
D. Quickly take to a self-serve, coin-operated dry cleaning machine.

Follow the Label

Name _____

Date _____ Period_____

Consumer performance claims for a garment are not valid unless the recommended care instructions have been followed. Using four of your own garments, provide the information requested below. Then fill in the additional information. "Your care of the items" should include specific types of laundering products, equipment settings, drying methods, etc. "Results" might include how nice or poor the garment looks, if it needs more ironing than expected, or if any shrinkage, discoloration, or pilling has occurred.

1. Garment: _____

   Care label information: _____

   _____

   _____

   Your care of the item: _____

   _____

   _____

   Did you follow the recommended care instructions? _____

   Results: _____

   _____

   _____

2. Garment: _____

   Care label information: _____

   _____

   _____

   Your care of the item: _____

   _____

   _____

   Did you follow the recommended care instructions? _____

   Results: _____

   _____

   _____

3. Garment: _____

   Care label information: _____

   _____

   _____

   Your care of the item: _____

   _____

   _____

(Continued)

Did you follow the recommended care instructions? _____

Results: _____

_____

_____

_____

4. Garment: _____

Care label information: _____

_____

_____

Your care of the item: _____

_____

_____

Did you follow the recommended care instructions? _____

Results: _____

_____

_____

Careers in the Textile Industry

Categorizing Jobs

Activity A

Chapter 19

Name _____

Date _____ Period_____

Match each employee with the general category of his or her job.

R = Research and development

D = Design

P = Production

M = Marketing and sales

A = Administration

_____ 1. Purchasing agent

_____ 2. Advertising/promotion agent

_____ 3. Converter

_____ 4. Plant engineer

_____ 5. Quality control inspector

_____ 6. Data processing employee

_____ 7. Industrial engineer

_____ 8. Personnel administrator

_____ 9. Market analyst

_____ 10. Textile stylist

_____ 11. Trainee

_____ 12. Textile colorist

_____ 13. Machine operator

_____ 14. Accounting/finance employee

_____ 15. Textile surface designer

_____ 16. Public relations agent

_____ 17. Research scientist

_____ 18. Sales manager

_____ 19. Business planner

_____ 20. Textile tester

_____ 21. Machine technician

_____ 22. Office manager

_____ 23. Laboratory technician

_____ 24. Sales representative

_____ 25. Production supervisor

_____ 26. Textile structural designer

After analyzing the answers, which general category appeals the most to you and why? _____

_____

_____

_____

Textile Careers

Name _____

Date _____ Period_____

Fill in the spaces with the correct terms.

1.					T	
2.					E	
3.					X	
4.					T	
5.					I	
6.					L	
7.					E	
8.					I	
9.					N	
10.					D	
11.					U	
12.					S	
13.					T	
14.					R	
15.					Y	
16.					C	
17.					A	
18.					R	
19.					E	
20.					E	
21.					R	
22.					S	

(Continued)

1. _____ processing employees use computers for such administrative operations as keeping track of sales, shipping, billing, inventories, employees' records, and the payroll.

2. Plant _____ keep all environmental systems, such as heating, air-conditioning, electrical, and materials handling, operating properly.

3. _____ testers are technicians who test new products against the specifications that must be met. They also perform tests during manufacturing to assure good and uniform quality.

4. _____ engineers are cost and efficiency experts who coordinate people, materials, equipment, space, and energy to save time and money for the firm.

5. The _____ of a company is concerned with the overall running, or managing, of it.

6. The career area of _____ refers to the exchange of goods from the supplier to the customer for money.

7. Machine _____ are production workers who run the machines that do the manufacturing procedures.

8. A(n) _____ manager is an administrative employee who supervises a particular office for a company.

9. A(n) _____ technician is a production employee who keeps the equipment in good working order.

10. _____ and promotion agents try to create a demand for the firm's products by telling customers that there is something wonderful to buy.

11. The _____ and finance department of a firm keeps track of the funds of the company.

12. _____ planners gather data on the company's operations, analyze it, and make recommendations of action to the company's management.

13. A case of loose, unfolded art or design papers showing a person's creative work is called a(n) _____.

14. _____ is the business of finding or creating a market for products. It includes pricing, promotion, and distribution at a profit.

15. A market _____ conducts market research by studying consumer tastes and changing trends to predict future demand for specific goods.

16. _____ supervisors coordinate and direct various manufacturing operations to maintain the highest production and the best quality.

17. _____ control inspectors analyze the quality of manufactured products and try to solve problems when necessary so salable goods are produced.

18. _____ decide how various amounts of fabrics should be dyed, printed, or otherwise finished.

19. _____ scientists are technical employees, usually with advanced degrees, who work in laboratories to discover new knowledge, develop new products, or improve existing products.

20. _____ jobs involve short-term independent work assignments done by an individual for various firms.

21. Textile _____ are employees who decide which color combinations to use in textile designs.

22. A(n) _____ administrator oversees the people employed by a firm, especially in regard to hiring, firing, and receiving pay and benefits.

After analyzing these careers, which specific one appeals the most to you and why? _____

_____

_____

_____

_____

_____

_____

_____

_____

_____

_____

Seeking Answers

Name _____

Date _____ Period_____

1. What does the textile industry do? _____

_____

_____

2. Name three specific textile majors offered by colleges and technical schools throughout the country. __

_____

_____

3. What is the purpose of "R & D"? _____

_____

_____

4. What personal requirements are recommended for a career in research and development?_____

_____

_____

5. What personal qualifications are recommended for a career in textile design? _____

_____

_____

6. Why are beginners advised not to seek freelance jobs? _____

_____

_____

7. What is the difference between a textile designer and a textile stylist? _____

_____

_____

8. Why do most firms encourage their management personnel to attend seminars, workshops, and selected classes? _____

_____

_____

9. Why are converters such key people in textile production? _____

_____

_____

10. Why do market analysts conduct market research?_____

_____

_____

A Closer Look

Activity D

Chapter 19

Name _____

Date _____ Period_____

Analyze and compare four different careers described in this chapter by filling out the following.

1. **Employee's title:** _____

   Preparation needed:_____

   _____

   _____

   Duties and responsibilities: _____

   _____

   _____

   Average salary or pay range: _____

   Typical work hours: _____

   Advantages: _____

   _____

   _____

   Disadvantages: _____

   _____

   _____

2. **Employee's title:** _____

   Preparation needed:_____

   _____

   _____

   Duties and responsibilities: _____

   _____

   _____

   Average salary or pay range: _____

   Typical work hours: _____

   Advantages: _____

   _____

   _____

   Disadvantages: _____

   _____

   _____

(Continued)

Name _____

3. **Employee's title:** _____

   Preparation needed: _____
   _____
   _____

   Duties and responsibilities: _____
   _____
   _____

   Average salary or pay range: _____

   Typical work hours: _____

   Advantages: _____
   _____
   _____

   Disadvantages: _____
   _____
   _____

4. **Employee's title:** _____

   Preparation needed: _____
   _____
   _____

   Duties and responsibilities: _____
   _____
   _____

   Average salary or pay range: _____

   Typical work hours: _____

   Advantages: _____
   _____
   _____

   Disadvantages: _____
   _____
   _____

Read and React

Activity E

Chapter 19

Name _____

Date _____ Period_____

Read the following true statements and indicate your reaction to each. Check if you think the statement is an interesting aspect of textile industry employment, if it seems uninteresting to you, or if you are unsure about it. You will not be graded on your reactions. Then choose the statement that you find the most interesting and explain your feelings in detail.

Interesting	Uninteresting	Unsure
_____	_____	_____
_____	_____	_____
_____	_____	_____
_____	_____	_____
_____	_____	_____
_____	_____	_____
_____	_____	_____
_____	_____	_____
_____	_____	_____
_____	_____	_____
_____	_____	_____

1. "Vertical companies," which are usually large firms, may do all operations from textile production to apparel manufacturing.
2. An "embroidery designer" is a specialist who does detailed technical drawings on graph paper or computer for designs of lace and embroidery textiles.
3. A "knit grapher" graphs instructions or does computer calculations for knit fabric designs.
4. Computer programs that are available for textile design work are so sophisticated that they offer over 4,000 colors with the ability to fade or brighten them as desired.
5. Textile experts used to think that the use of computers would not be effective for design work. However, most now agree that computers have decreased the fatigue of design employees and have expanded the industry's creative horizons.
6. Textiles are not just for apparel. They also have countless household, industrial, and medical applications. There are 25,000 textile products made for the military alone!
7. In the textile industry, computers are used not only for design, but are also important for research, production, marketing, sales, and administrative duties.
8. About one million jobs deal directly with textile production, making approximately 25 billion square yards of fabric each year. The majority is used in apparel.
9. The United States consumes more textile products than any other country with an average of over 6 pounds per person each year.
10. The same job title covers different duties in different textile firms depending on company size, specialty, management, organization, and philosophy.
11. Many commodity, or basic, textiles are no longer made in the United States. They can be mass-produced much more cheaply overseas, so the American industry has become flexible to make shorter runs of fashion fabrics instead.

(Continued)

_____   _____   _____   12. Demographics tell us that by the year 2000, over half of Americans will be over 50 years old. This "aging of the population" is causing textile researchers to develop specific fabrics for the comfort and lifestyles of the older, active, fashionable adult market.

_____   _____   _____   13. Extremely thin microdenier manufactured fibers can be tightly woven into light, soft raincoat fabrics that are wind and rain resistant, yet luxurious.

_____   _____   _____   14. Corporate attire has become more casual, with many male and female managers and executives shedding their business suits for slacks or skirts and sweaters. Such trends are noticed by textile manufacturers who then shift their production away from pin-striped suitings to less formal fabrics.

_____   _____   _____   15. Textiles have a "product life cycle" just like fashions and other consumer products. The cycle stages include introduction, growth, maturity, and decline. Saturation occurs and substitutes become available at the end, after which consumers lose interest and firms change to the production of other textiles.

_____   _____   _____   16. The manufactured fiber segment is the most "capital intensive" of the textile/apparel pipeline. In other words, it requires larger investments in plants, machinery, and equipment than textile mills, apparel manufacturers, or retailers.

The most interesting statement is #_____ because _____

_____

_____

_____

_____

_____

_____

_____

_____

_____

_____

_____

_____

_____

_____

_____

_____

_____

Job Titles and Descriptions

Activity A

Chapter 20

Name _____

Date _____ Period_____

In the blank beside each job description, write the corresponding job title. Then complete the exercise on the following page.

_____

_____

_____

_____

_____

_____

_____

_____

_____

_____

_____

_____

_____

_____

1. Records a season's line of designs in precise technical illustrations for the company's records.
2. Cuts around pattern pieces, making the garment parts needed for production.
3. Does whatever hand sewing is needed to finish garments in better-quality, higher-priced apparel lines.
4. Repairs defects that have occurred to garments during factory production.
5. Translates an apparel design into pattern pieces that can be used for mass production.
6. Makes illustration-quality drawings of the ideas that a designer has draped in fabric onto a dressmaker's form.
7. Figures out how the garment pattern pieces can be placed most efficiently, in the tightest possible layout, for cutting.
8. Constructs garments on heavy, fast, industrial power sewing machines.
9. Lays out the chosen fabric for cutting.
10. Creates new ideas for garments and accessories.
11. Checks garment parts during production, as well as finished garments, for flaws and imperfections.
12. Cuts patterns in all of the different sizes to be produced.
13. Sews the designer's sample garment together, testing the pattern in fabric.
14. Sorts and prepares the cut garment parts to go through progressive bundle production.
15. Gains on-the-job learning experience while working under a fashion designer.
16. Determines the overall price of producing each apparel item.

(Continued)

_____

_____

_____

_____

_____

_____

_____

_____

17. Does detail work and record keeping for the plant manager.
18. Directs sewing machine operators and other factory workers to achieve the highest quality and speed of production.
19. Researches and buys the fabrics, trims, and notions for an apparel manufacturing firm.
20. Oversees every aspect (design, manufacture, selling, and delivery) of a product line or a specific category of items within a line.
21. Develops specifications for items that will be manufactured and makes sure those standards are met during all production phases.
22. Has responsibility for all operations at a plant site.
23. Instructs new operators how to do specific tasks or use specialized machines.
24. Makes "outside" sales presentations of the company's line away from the firm's sales office and showroom.
25. Makes "in house" sales presentations of a line of goods to buyers who visit the manufacturer's showroom.

Review the job titles and descriptions above and tell which one appeals the most to you and why. _____

_____

_____

_____

_____

_____

_____

_____

_____

_____

_____

_____

_____

_____

_____

_____

_____

_____

_____

_____

You as a Designer

Name _____

Date _____ Period_____

Assume the identity of a designer of ladies' sportswear, women's evening gowns, men's sportswear, boys' beach-wear, or other category of your choice. Draw original creations on the figures here. Then tell why you included the particular features of your designs.

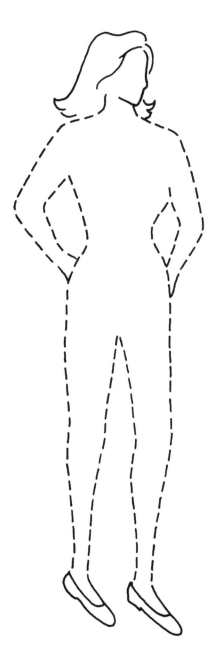

1. _____

_____

_____

_____

_____

_____

_____

_____

_____

_____

_____

_____

_____

_____

_____

_____

_____

_____

_____

_____

_____

_____

_____

_____

_____

_____

(Continued)

Name _____

2. _____
_____
_____
_____
_____
_____
_____
_____
_____
_____
_____
_____
_____
_____
_____
_____
_____
_____
_____
_____
_____
_____
_____
_____

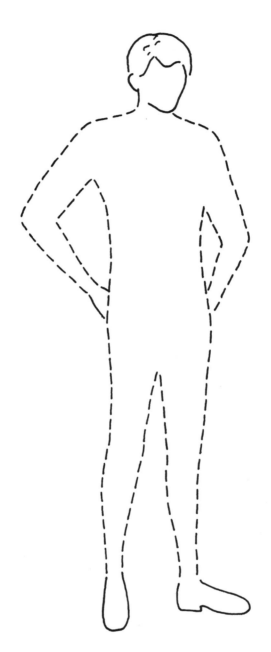

A Sales Presentation

Activity C

Chapter 20

Name _____

Date _____ Period_____

Think about the communication skills and personal style needed to make a successful sales presentation. Assume the identity of a showroom salesperson or a traveling sales rep. Describe your apparel line here. How might you present it to gain the highest possible number of sales? What are the newest styling features, fabrics, and colors that you would stress? What suggestions might you make about ways retailers could present and display the merchandise? How would you handle objections? How might you close the sale?

_____
_____
_____
_____
_____
_____
_____
_____
_____
_____
_____
_____
_____
_____
_____
_____
_____
_____
_____
_____
_____
_____
_____
_____
_____
_____
_____
_____

Qualifications for Careers

Name _____

Date _____ Period _____

Match each of the following job titles with the person whose qualifications meet it best.

_____ 1. Ron has worked hard at his sales rep job and has a long, successful record of achievement. With this experience and his knowledge of the field, he is ready to take on more responsibility in the firm.

_____ 2. Cho-lee has studied the fashion field and would like to get into apparel sales with a manufacturer. She plans to move to New York City, Los Angeles, or another fashion center. She realizes she could learn a great deal by working under experienced people.

_____ 3. Jessica enjoys calculating operational methods and the corresponding machinery that will give the best production performance. She gets excited about finding the best way to do something using the least amount of time and motion. She wants to be part of the fashion world even though she is getting a college degree in a technical field.

_____ 4. Philippe likes the concept of moving merchandise from one place to another according to a plan. It gives him a feeling of satisfaction to know that the right amounts of the right merchandise get to each retail store.

_____ 5. Scott has a high school diploma but no advanced education. He lives near some apparel manufacturing plants and is willing to learn on the job. During an employment interview, he made it clear that he has good tolerance for standing, steam, heat, and noise.

_____ 6. After finishing some higher education, Maureen is just starting out in the apparel field. She has always enjoyed fabrics, trims, and notions. She is happiest if she can get them at bargain prices, since she has a good eye for value. She doesn't mind doing clerical duties in order to prepare for a more responsible position in the future.

_____ 7. Karen is a self-employed sales rep who handles women's exercise apparel lines for several small manufacturers. She sells a line of leotards from one manufacturer, sweat suits from another, socks and sweat bands from another, and specially designed undergarments from another.

_____ 8. Tom has had a successful career with many positions of responsibility that he has handled very well. He has just been named to head the company.

_____ 9. Ben has education and experience with computers as well as a good "feel" for fashion. His job combines these skills to advise sales employees to stress particular items or colors in various parts of the country.

_____ 10. After being a top-notch showroom salesperson, Shawna has recently been promoted. She enjoys her supervisory duties and makes sure that everything is prepared perfectly for buyers' visits.

A. administrative employee

B. assistant designer

C. assistant piece goods buyer

D. C.E.O.

E. copyist

F. costing engineer

G. distribution employee

H. division director

I. finisher

J. industrial engineer

K. jobber

L. merchandise control specialist

M. pattern grader

N. plant engineer

O. presser

P. product manager

Q. quality control engineer

R. sales manager

S. showroom manager

T. showroom sales trainee

U. sketching assistant

V. training supervisor

_____11. Hilario enjoys the challenge of keeping the apparel production factory where he works operating smoothly. He maintains the facility's heating, lighting, noise reduction, and other environmental operations.

_____12. During Kate's many years with the firm, she has learned to make important decisions accurately and to lead others with confidence. She does a good job of coordinating the operations of the product managers, plant managers, and sales managers under her.

_____13. Sandra is an accounting and finance specialist. She enjoys working in an office and mixing with others who do personnel, data processing, and public relations work.

_____14. Terry is a new employee in the design department of a large firm that produces mass amounts of lower-priced items. Most of his work involves adapting higher-priced designs to meet the price range of his firm's customers. After he gains experience in this job, he hopes to move up to a more creative position with a higher-priced line.

_____15. Faith aspires to be a successful fashion designer someday. However, she just graduated from college and needs some working experience to learn the "ins and outs" of the career. This entry-level job will give her an apprenticeship opportunity and a chance to start proving herself.

_____16. Tanya lives near an exclusive wedding gown manufacturer that makes high-quality items by special order. Although she cannot sketch or make patterns, Tanya thinks the hand sewing skills taught to her by her grandmother might enable her to work for the firm.

_____17. Robert has always been a perfectionist and likes products that meet high standards. He has a knack for knowing how to attain expected levels of performance and wonders how he can use this aptitude if combined with education.

_____18. Vince has always had a flare for art. However, rather than doing abstract paintings, his drawings have always been realistic, precise, and detailed. His family is moving to a large city with many apparel firms and he is hoping to be able to find a job with a manufacturing company.

_____19. Carol has worked for a firm as the assistant piece goods buyer and as an assistant to the plant's industrial engineer. She is familiar with the prices of fabrics and notions used to produce the company's garments as well as the production processes necessary to produce them. She is good with numbers, and a management job is now opening up that she would like to apply for.

_____20. Since completing trade school, Maria has worked at almost all of the sewing operations in an apparel manufacturing plant. She knows all about the tasks done on specialized machines and is ready to be promoted. The plant manager has the perfect job in mind for her.

Doing Market Research

Name _____

Date _____ Period_____

Research an apparel area such as men's sports shirts, ladies' dresses, juniors' slacks, boys' sweaters, or another category. Prepare a list of questions to which the answers would be of interest to a manufacturer of the garments. Ask the questions to a cross section (representative sample) of the people who would buy the garment. Look for articles in newspapers or magazines to help you with your analysis of consumers' habits, needs, and wants. Write a report about your findings that would help the manufacturer design and produce garments to match the upcoming market demand.

_____

_____

_____

_____

_____

_____

_____

_____

_____

_____

_____

_____

_____

_____

_____

_____

_____

_____

_____

_____

_____

_____

_____

_____

_____

_____

_____

_____

_____

_____

_____

Fashion Merchandising and Other Retail Industry Careers

Select an Occupation

Activity A

Chapter 21

Name _____

Date _____ Period_____

1. If you were to have a retail career, check the area that you would prefer:

   _____ Merchandise planning and buying

   _____ Direct selling

   _____ Store operations

   _____ Retail management

   Why? _____

   _____

   _____

   _____

2. What training would you seek to prepare yourself for this work? _____

   _____

   _____

   _____

3. What entry-level job would you expect? _____

   _____

   _____

   _____

4. To what job would you aspire for the peak of your career? _____

   _____

   _____

   _____

5. What job duties would you expect to have, and what skills do you think you would perfect between your career's entry and peak? _____

   _____

   _____

   _____

A Diamond of Retail Occupations

Activity B

Chapter 21

Name _____

Date _____ Period_____

Read the numbered definitions and write the terms in the corresponding spaces in the diamond.

1. The _____ of stock is responsible for all stock functions and coordinates the activities of the stock clerks.
2. A retail _____ is responsible for selecting and purchasing goods and for selling the items at a profit for a department or division of a store or retail business.
3. A(n) _____ manager is an administrative employee who supervises a particular office for a company.
4. A(n) _____ agent is an office worker who keeps track of monetary amounts due and sends out bills for those amounts.
5. A(n) _____ service manager is in charge of handling complaints and returns as well as special needs, such as gift wrapping, home delivery, and special orders.
6. A retail employee who receives on-the-job training for potential buyer and management postions is called a(n) _____ trainee.
7. _____ shoppers shop in their own stores and in competitive stores to examine the merchandise, prices, and customer services.
8. _____ are employees who record and summarize business transactions and report the results.
9. _____/planners keep track of merchandise and allocate various stock items to the branches of retail chains that need them.
10. A(n) _____ _____ is a retail executive responsible for the profitable operation of an entire store and all its functions.
11. A(n) _____ buyer selects and purchases one category of goods for a large retail organization.
12. A(n) _____ _____ office buyer provides market buying help for member store buyers.
13. A(n) _____ _____, or fashion consultant, selects merchandise for customers.
14. A(n) _____ _____ coordinator helps the fashion coordinator in many different ways.
15. A(n) _____ _____ does the sewing to take in, let out, and reshape garments, so they fit the customers who buy them.
16. A(n) _____ _____ is responsible for the total business coordination of several departments or an entire branch store.

17. A(n) _____ _____ deals directly with customers by selling merchandise, preparing sales checks, and receiving payments for the sales.
18. _____ _____ collect and record customers' payments and bag the merchandise after finalizing each sale.
19. _____ _____ buyers help buyers with many different tasks as they work to gain the knowledge and experience needed to become buyers.
20. A(n) _____ _____ answers telephones, schedules appointments, follows up on shipments, does filing, and handles other matters to help a retail buyer.
21. A(n) _____ _____ protects records, customers, employees, and property against theft or harm.
22. Fashion _____ _____ is the planning, buying, and selling of apparel and other fashion items.
23. _____ buyers plan and buy all the goods for the department they manage in a traditional department store.
24. _____ workers clean, paint, and repair the physical structures of a business.
25. A training _____ gives orientation classes to new salespeople and updating programs to current salespeople.
26. The _____ director oversees the hiring and firing of employees as well as the fringe benefit programs.
27. A big advantage to retail employment is the 10 percent to 25 percent _____ on personal purchases made at the store.
28. A(n) _____ coordinator ties together the merchandise of various departments, organizes in-store fashion promotions, and keeps employees updated on the latest fashion trends.
29. A(n) _____ coordinator coordinates several branch stores of a company.
30. _____ clerks receive and mark merchandise, move it to the selling floor, maintain inventory records, and otherwise handle merchandise inventory.

(Continued)

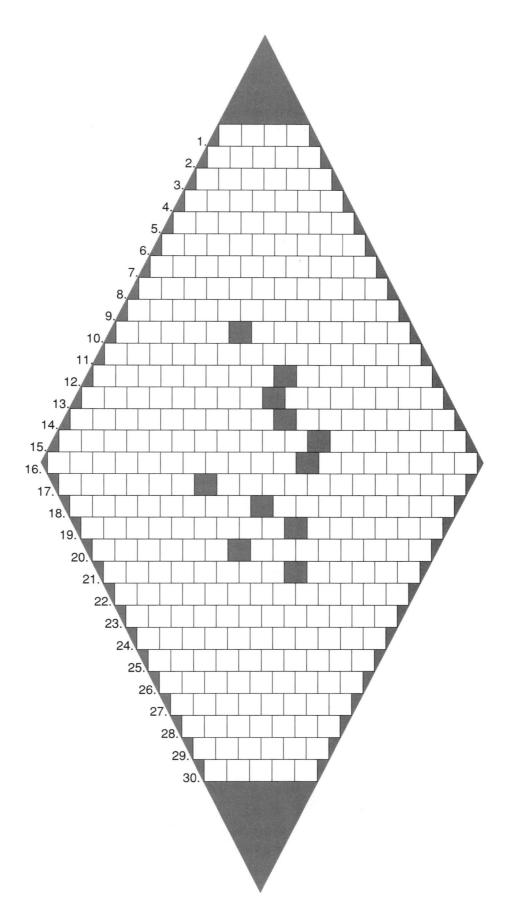

The Retail Ladder Game

Activity C

Chapter 21

Name _____

Date _____ Period_____

To play, two or three players should use small buttons or colored pieces of paper as markers. Roll one die each turn to determine the number of spaces to advance. Move back and forth across the board following the direction of the arrows and numbers. Notice that the positions gain in pay and status as the players proceed upward, but not necessarily in a straight career path.

To determine which player starts, roll the die. The player with the highest number begins with a new roll. Two players can land on the same space, but the third player to land there must skip his or her turn instead of moving there. The first player to reach "Top Management" with an exact roll of the die is the winner.

76	77	ASSISTANT STORE MANAGER 78	79	LOW SALES– LOSE 2 TURNS 80	81	PAY RAISE– ADVANCE 3 SPACES 82
75						
MERCHANDISE MANAGER 74	73	72	FASHION COORDINATOR 71	70	GO BACK TO RETAIL BUYER (59) 69	68

46	47	GOOD WORK– ADVANCE 1 SPACE 48	49	50	HEAD OF STOCK 51	52
PERSONAL SHOPPER 45						
44	ASSISTANT BUYER 43	42	RECORD SALES– TAKE ANOTHER TURN 41	40	COMPARISON SHOPPER 39	MOVE UP TO HEAD OF STOCK (51) 38

RETAIL SALESPERSON 16	17	DIPLOMA– MOVE TO EXECUTIVE TRAINEE (31) 18	19	20	SECURITY GUARD 21	22
15						
14	GO BACK TO STOCK CLERK (6) 13	12	11	MAINTENANCE WORKER 10	9	8

176   Chapter 21   Fashion Merchandising and Other Retail Industry Careers   Copyright Goodheart-Willcox Co., Inc.

| 99 | 100 | 101 | 102 MUST PROVE YOURSELF–GO BACK 4 SPACES | 103 | 104 | – TOP MANAGEMENT – |

| 98 |

| 97 | 96 BRANCH COORDINATOR | 95 | 94 | 93 PERSONNEL DIRECTOR | 92 | 91 |

| | | | | | | 90 |

| 83 | 84 | 85 | 86 STORE MANAGER (WOW!) | 87 | 88 | 89 ↑ |

| 67 | 66 TRAINING SUPERVISOR (AN EXPERT!) | 65 | 64 | 63 BAD JUDGEMENT– GO BACK 3 SPACES | 62 | 61 |

| | | | | | | 60 |

| 53 CUSTOMER SERVICE MANAGER | 54 | 55 | 56 | 57 | 58 ASSISTANT FASHION COORDINATOR | 59 RETAIL BUYER ↑ |

| 37 | 36 | 35 | 34 OFFICE WORKER | 33 | 32 | 31 EXECUTIVE TRAINEE |

| | | | | | | 30 |

| 23 | 24 LATE TO WORK–LOSE 1 TURN | 25 ALTERATIONS EXPERT | 26 | 27 | 28 | 29 ↑ |

| 7 | 6 STOCK CLERK (NICE ENTRY) | 5 START OVER NEXT TURN | 4 | 3 CHECKOUT CASHIER (GOOD START) | 2 | 1 ← START |

Thoughts on Retail Employment

Activity D

Chapter 21

Name _____

Date _____ Period_____

1. Describe what is involved in fashion merchandising. _____

   _____

   _____

   _____

   _____

2. What has caused the recent reduction to fewer, but larger, retail stores? _____

   _____

   _____

   _____

   _____

3. Why has the number of retail jobs available stopped growing? _____

   _____

   _____

   _____

   _____

4. Why are jobs in large stores and retail chains more specialized than jobs in small shops?_____

   _____

   _____

   _____

   _____

5. Name at least five character traits that are recommended for a person who plans to go into retail work.

   _____

   _____

   _____

   _____

6. Name at least five specific courses included in fashion merchandising or retailing curricula. _____

   _____

   _____

   _____

   _____

   _____

Careers in Fashion Promotion

Career Categorizing

Activity A   Name _____

Chapter 22   Date _____ Period_____

For each category listed on the left, circle the word or phrase among the rest that does not fit according to the textbook. Then, on the lines provided, explain why the circled word or phrase does not fit.

1. **fashion advertising**   graphic designer   art director   public relations agent   account executive

   _____

   _____

   _____

2. **fashion promotion**   direct selling   advertising work   indirect selling   display work

   _____

   _____

   _____

3. **fashion photography**   film   camera   props   drawings

   _____

   _____

   _____

4. **fashion modeling**   runway work   display work   mannequin work   photography work

   _____

   _____

   _____

5. **fashion journalism**   editor   copywriter   model   audio-visual work

   _____

   _____

   _____

Freelance Employment

Activity B

Chapter 22

Name _____

Date _____ Period_____

Define freelance work: _____
_____
_____
_____

Check which career would interest you the most as a freelancer:

_____ fashion photographer   _____ fashion illustrator   _____ fashion model

Research it from a freelance perspective and answer the following questions.

1. What education would you need? _____
_____
_____

2. What preparatory work experience would you seek?_____
_____
_____

3. How would you establish the rates you would charge? _____
_____
_____

4. How would you keep records and do billing? _____
_____
_____

5. How would you negotiate contracts with clients? _____
_____
_____

6. Are there any other legal aspects you should consider? _____
_____
_____

7. How would you develop leads for jobs and market your service?_____
_____
_____

8. What kind of a portfolio would you assemble to promote your work?_____
_____
_____

Fashion Journalism

Activity C

Chapter 22

Name _____

Date _____ Period_____

Assume the identity of a fashion writer. Research general fashion trends at your school and write an article about them. If you wish, submit the article for publication in your school or community newspaper.

Research:

Fads this year: _____

_____

_____

Newest colors: _____

_____

_____

Lasting styles still popular: _____

_____

_____

Fashionable fabrics and textures: _____

_____

_____

Noteworthy accessories: _____

_____

_____

Other facts to note: _____

_____

_____

Article:

Fashion News at

_____

(your school)

_____

_____

_____

_____

_____

_____

_____

_____

_____

(Continued)

Truths and Falsehoods

Activity D

Chapter 22

Name _____

Date _____ Period_____

Write either *True* or *False* in front of each of the statements below.

_____ 1. People in indirect selling jobs show, draw, model, photograph, write about, and talk about fashions.

_____ 2. Most art directors are employed directly by producers of nationally distributed textiles or apparel.

_____ 3. Computers are seldom used in advertising graphics and typesetting because of the creative flow of artistic expression needed.

_____ 4. Some vocational schools offer specific programs in display design.

_____ 5. Display managers are mainly in charge of getting broadcast advertising time for their firm and its products.

_____ 6. When fashion illustration work is done for a pattern company, exotic background touches are added to help convince customers to buy.

_____ 7. Fashion modeling is done either in front of live audiences or in front of cameras.

_____ 8. Fashion models have unpredictable employment and irregular earnings.

_____ 9. Models must have good health and physical stamina.

_____ 10. Large businesses almost always hire models through modeling agencies.

_____ 11. Photographers may take pictures of fashion apparel on live models or still shots of fashion merchandise.

_____ 12. Photo stylists test the lighting, take sample photos, and work with darkroom equipment.

_____ 13. Editors set policy and give out assignments, since they are administrators as well as journalists.

_____ 14. Audio-visual work involves planning programs, writing scripts, getting props, and producing or being in the presentations.

_____ 15. Public relations agents try to buy the best advertising or promotional print space or broadcast time for their firms.

_____ 16. Graphic designers come up with what is needed for advertisements and collateral materials based on the ideas of the art director.

_____ 17. Layout artists formulate interesting backgrounds for models to stand near in fashion photographs.

_____ 18. Display designers usually gear their work toward special events or promotional activities.

_____ 19. Mannequin work is modeling for fashion illustration courses that draw live figures.

_____ 20. Copywriters sometimes write descriptions of garments for mail-order catalogs.

_____ 21. Some fashion photographers shoot motion footage on film or videotape.

_____ 22. Photography is considered to be one of the least flexible forms of artistic expression in fashion communication.

_____ 23. Fashion writers send out press kits to manufacturers and advertisers in hopes of being hired by them.

_____ 24. Publicity is an expensive, but effective, type of promotion.

Add the Words

Chapter 22

Name _____

Date _____ Period_____

Fill in the missing words from the following paragraphs. Then complete the exercise below.

Fashion (1) __ __ __ __ __ __ __ __ __ , or indirect (2) __ __ __ __ __ __ __ , offers many exciting career opportunities.

People who work in the fashion (3) __ __ __ __ __ __ __ __ __ __ __ __ field try to sell products by creating attractive, informative ads. Agency employees in charge of handling specific accounts are called account (4) __ __ __ __ __ __ __ __ __ __ __. Designers who conceptualize the ads are usually called (5) __ __ __ __ __ __ __ __ __ __ __. Their ideas become reality by the (6) __ __ __ __ __ __ __ designers who may have been promoted from (7) __ __ __ __ __ __ __ artist (who does the "comp" renderings) or (8) __ __ __ __ __ - __ __ / __ __ __ __ __ __ __ __ __ __ artist (who puts together the various art and copy elements of the ads).

In other employment fields, fashion (9) __ __ __ __ __ __ __ __ __ __ __ __ __ __ do drawings of garments. If they are good and become well-known, they sometimes decide to be independent (10) __ __ __ __ __ __ __ __ artists. To be hired in this field, a(n) (11) __ __ __ __ __ __ __ __ __ containing examples of the artist's work is needed.

Fashion (12) __ __ __ __ __ __ wear apparel to show it off. When working in the showroom of a manufacturer, it is usually called (13) __ __ __ __ __ __ __ __ __ __ work. If it is done in front of cameras, it is called (14) __ __ __ __ __ __ __ __ __ __ __ work. Fashion (15) __ __ __ __ __ __ __ __ __ __ __ __ __ take pictures. Their apprentices, who are getting on-the-job experience, are called (16) __ . There are also employees who book models, pick up and return garments and props, and accessorize and iron the apparel. They are called (17) __ __ __ __ __ __ __ __ __ __ __ __ __ __ .

Fashion (18) __ __ __ __ __ __ __ are journalists who work for newspapers and magazines. Sometimes manufacturers and advertisers send them press (19) __ __ __ __ , or releases, as a source of information for their articles. An administrative job in this field is that of (20) __ __ __ __ __ __ __.

21. Write your own paragraph about a career aspect in fashion promotion.

_____

_____

_____

_____

_____

_____

_____

_____

_____

_____

_____

Other Careers and Entrepreneurial Opportunities

Unscramble and Use

Activity A   Name _____

Chapter 23   Date _____ Period_____

Unscramble the following terms that are italicized in Chapter 23 of the textbook. Then write a sentence using each term correctly as it relates to the content of the chapter.

1. TOSMECU TORRACU _____ _____

   _____

   _____

   _____

2. TOARPRONCIO _____

   _____

   _____

   _____

3. YOTNUC SIEEONNXT GATNE _____ _____ _____

   _____

   _____

   _____

4. SNIBSUES LANP _____ _____

   _____

   _____

   _____

5. RENERPERTUNE _____

   _____

   _____

   _____

(Continued)

Name _____

6. ATAUCOIDENL NESRETAPETVIRE _____ _____

_____
_____
_____

7. RADNIGT CAYMOPN _____ _____

_____
_____
_____

8. REFEGACLNIN _____

_____
_____
_____

9. HAPPENRRSTI _____

_____
_____
_____

10. LCNGNTSIUO _____

_____
_____
_____

11. NIGOCNTEMNS _____

_____
_____
_____

12. CAAEIHLRTT IOUCGMNST _____ _____

_____
_____
_____

13. GACETOT STRINDYU _____ _____

_____
_____
_____

14. LOSE PRPRPRTOSOHIIE _____ _____

_____
_____
_____

Read and React

Name _____

Date _____ Period _____

Think about the following statements and write your reaction to each on the lines provided.

1. The major pattern companies consider letters from their customers (with requests, questions, complaints, or praise) to be their best source of market information. Members of their consumer services staffs answer all of the thousands of letters and phone calls they receive annually. _____

   _____

   _____

   _____

   _____

2. Sometimes creative people who like to be in a theatrical environment volunteer to help with the costumes for school or community amateur productions. Through experience, training, and contacts, they may work into careers doing the costuming for major stage productions or opera companies. _____

   _____

   _____

   _____

   _____

3. In the past decade there has been a boom in entrepreneurship. Small businesses dominate the American economy. Seventy percent of all retailers have less than four paid employees, and there are about 600 small manufacturers for every large producer. However, a large number of small businesses fail, usually because of poor planning and incompetence. _____

   _____

   _____

   _____

   _____

4. Some people think that high schools and trade schools should teach only mass production sewing methods, such as sewing with sergers. Even those who do home sewing in the future, or run small tailor/seamstress shops, will probably use these methods rather than the old single-stitching and hand finishing methods. _____

   _____

   _____

   _____

   _____

(Continued)

5. Extension agents can offer many educational aids through workshops, leaflets, slide sets, sample kits, and access to experts. Their help is generally inexpensive or free. Your county extension office is often listed in the community service section of your local phone book. _____

_____

_____

_____

6. In many communities, there is a demand for "private conservators." As self-employed costume restorers, these people clean antique garments and wedding gowns without using harmful solvents. They remove any toxins, stabilize the garments, wrap them in washed, unbleached cotton, and pack them in acid-free boxes for storage. _____

_____

_____

_____

7. The U.S. Small Business Administration has about 100 different booklets on specific subjects to help entrepreneurs plan their businesses and keep them running smoothly. A free list, which includes ordering instructions, can be obtained from the nearest office. _____

_____

_____

_____

8. Apparel design and manufacturing entrepreneurs should have unique and salable concepts as well as the willingness to pay their "dues" in time, money, and effort. They must dismiss the ill-conceived impression that it's all fun and games, fame and fortune, and glamour and glitter! _____

_____

_____

_____

9. A popular entrepreneurial business venture is the rental of formal wear and wedding attire. This is a good niche, because consumers don't want to purchase such expensive garments that may only be worn once.

_____

_____

_____

_____

Find Your Entrepreneurial Aptitude

Activity C

Chapter 23

Name _____

Date _____ Period_____

Studies have shown that two specific traits are possessed by people who become successful entrepreners. A high degree of nerve (confidence with courage) enables people to control their environment rather than to be controlled by it. A strong urge for achievement motivates them to show their effectiveness and gain success. To calculate your aptitude, respond to the statements below. Place your scores in the appropriate columns. Give yourself 4 points if you strongly agree with the statement, 3 points if you generally agree, 2 points if you disagree somewhat, and I point if you strongly disagree. Total your overall score to determine your entrepreneurial aptitude. You will not be graded on your responses. Then answer the question at the end of the activity.

Nerve:	I strongly agree (4 points)	I generally agree (3 points)	I disagree somewhat (2 points)	I strongly disagree (1 point)
1. I can do almost anything I set my mind to do.				
2. What happens to me in the future depends on me.				
3. I feel that my effort can successfully influence the outcome of a project.				
4. I can bring a change to many of the important things in my life.				
5. I rarely feel helpless in dealing with the prolems of life.				
6. I don't let myself be pushed around.				
Subtotals				

Urge for Achievement:	I strongly agree (4 points)	I generally agree (3 points)	I disagree somewhat (2 points)	I strongly disagree (1 point)
7. I always work hard to be the best one in any work or activity.				
8. It is hard for me to forget about my work when I'm away from it.				
9. I find it hard to totally relax when on vacation.				
10. I would rather work with a difficult, highly-competent partner than with a congenial, less-competent one.				
11. I feel angry when I see waste or inefficiency on the job.				
12. I am annoyed when people are late for appointments.				
Subtotals				

Total score: _____

If your total score is between 36 and 48, you have a high aptitude for becoming a successful entrepreneur. If your total score is between 24 and 35, you could probably be successful with your own business, but it might be difficult for you. If your total score is under 24, you would probably be more comfortable as an employee than as the owner of a business.

How does your score correspond with your previous thoughts about being an entrepreneur? _____

_____

_____

_____

_____

_____

_____

Planning Your Own Business

Activity D

Chapter 23

Name _____

Date _____ Period_____

Since initial planning can determine future success or failure, complete the following exercise to consider the challenge of becoming an entrepreneur. This type of thinking is needed before drafting the necessary business plan and seeking financing (capital) to actually start a business.

1. Does the idea of starting and operating your own business appeal to you? _____ If so, why? _____

    _____

    _____

    _____

2. If you had your own business, what specific products and/or services would you sell?_____

    _____

    _____

    _____

3. Describe the potential customers to whom you would market your products or services. _____

    _____

    _____

    _____

4. What competition would you have to consider or overcome? _____

    _____

    _____

    _____

5. What other problems, such as government regulations, changing demand, the development of better technology, etc., might confront you? _____

    _____

    _____

    _____

6. What personal strengths and weaknesses of yours, such as talents, energy, selling aptitude, and time to devote to all aspects, etc., should be considered before starting the business? _____

    _____

    _____

    _____

7   What education or training would you need before starting the business? How or where would you get it?

    _____

    _____

    _____

    _____

(Continued)

8. What would your expenses for rent, equipment, supplies, advertising, insurance, payroll, transportation, taxes and other fees, etc., be for starting and continuing to operate the business?

Expense category	Estimated costs

9. Based on all the above answers, what are the pros and cons of starting your own business?

Pros	Cons

10. If you would like to start your own business, describe your goals, business location, promotion strategy, and other ideas about it.

_____

_____

_____

_____

_____

_____

_____

_____

_____

_____

_____

_____

_____

Categorizing Occupations

Activity E

Chapter 23

Name _____

Date _____ Period_____

Place four job titles from the following list in each of the general categories below. Use each of the job titles one time. Then put an asterisk (*) before the job titles that require a college education and a pound sign (#) before the job titles that probably only require a high school diploma. Some job titles will not have a symbol in front of them, since they fall between the two, such as an associate degree or trade school.

Layout designer

Finisher

Fabric salesperson

Adult education teacher

Sole proprietor

Laundry specialist

Classroom teacher

Illustrator

Technical writer

Educational representative

Diagram artist

Spotter

Wardrobe designer

Design director

Freelancer

Pattern grader

Fitting model

County extension agent

Costume curator

Wrapper

Consultant

Checker

Mail-order business owner

Fabric editor

1. **Educators**

_____

_____

_____

_____

2. **Commercial Pattern Development**

_____

_____

_____

_____

3. **Pattern Guide Sheet and Envelope Production**

_____

_____

_____

_____

4. **Dry Cleaning Businesses**

_____

_____

_____

_____

5. **Entrepreneurs**

_____

_____

_____

_____

6. **Other**

_____

_____

_____

_____

Follow Your Interests

Activity F

Chapter 23

Name _____

Date _____ Period _____

Rate these general fashion career categories from 1 to 6 according to your interest with 1 being your highest interest and 6 being your lowest interest.

_____ Education

_____ Home sewing industry

_____ Textile and clothing historian

_____ Theatrical costuming

_____ Clothing care

_____ Entrepreneur

Choose a specific occupation that interests you from the category you marked as being your highest interest. Research that occupation and try to interview someone in that career. Write a brief report about it here and give an informative presentation to the class.

_____

_____

_____

_____

_____

_____

_____

_____

_____

_____

_____

_____

_____

_____

_____

_____

_____

_____

_____

_____

_____

_____

_____

A Career for You

Definition Match-Up

Activity A

Chapter 24

Name _____

Date _____ Period_____

Match the following definitions with the terms by placing the correct letter next to each number.

_____ 1. A person's natural talent or suitability to an activity.

_____ 2. A knowledge of what is happening.

_____ 3. A short business letter sent with a resume to express interest in interviewing for a job.

_____ 4. A public or privately-run office whose staff tries to match available jobs with qualified job applicants.

_____ 5. Specific training programs in trade schools that take one to three years to complete.

_____ 6. A deep conviction of your own worth or value.

_____ 7. A cooperative pairing of services, such as a school in a fashion center offering parts of its program for credit to university students away from the fashion scene.

_____ 8. Activities not falling within the regular academic scope of the curriculum, such as clubs and athletic programs.

_____ 9. Advertisements in newspapers and trade publications listed by classifications or subject groupings.

_____ 10. The devotion of a person's time and enthusiasm to a job, company, person, or cause.

_____ 11. A method of payment for employees in sales careers. It is a percentage of the dollar amount of sales made.

_____ 12. A collection of art or design papers showing a person's creative work.

_____ 13. Extra compensation, other than pay, such as paid vacation time, insurance, sick leave, and pension plans.

_____ 14. The energy and persistence to accomplish goals.

_____ 15. A face-to-face meeting between a job applicant and the person who hires employees for a company.

_____ 16. A paper requesting personal, academic, and employment information to be filled out by a job applicant.

_____ 17. Safeguards provided to workers by labor unions, government legislation, and private agencies.

_____ 18. The ability to always account for your own behavior and decisions.

_____ 19. Training in which schools place students in temporary jobs that relate to and alternate with their studies.

_____ 20. The ability to get along with others and to help them do tasks.

A. self-esteem

B. dedication

C. extracurricular

D. application form

E. awareness

F. commission

G. cooperation

H. networking

I. high ethics

J. aptitude

K. drive

L. portfolio

M. sense of responsibility

N. reciprocal agreement

O. reliability

P. employee protection

Q. job interview.

R. cover letter

S. communication skills

T. accomplishments

U. work-study program

V. certificate courses

W. classified ads

X. fringe benefits

Y. apprenticeship

Z. employment agency

Differentiate

Name _____

Date _____ Period_____

What is the difference between:

1. Hourly wage and salary? _____

_____

_____

_____

2. Associate degree and bachelor's degree? _____

_____

_____

_____

3. Placement office and personnel office? _____

_____

_____

_____

4. Resume and application form?_____

_____

_____

_____

5. Mentor and reference? _____

_____

_____

_____

6. Performance test and written test? _____

_____

_____

_____

7. Job interviewing and networking?_____

_____

_____

_____

8. Portfolio and transcript? _____

_____

_____

_____

Read and Think About It

Name _____

Date _____ Period_____

Read each of the following cases. Then write your thoughts and reactions on the lines provided.

1. Walt thinks that he might change his mind and want a career that does not fit with the college major he is in now. However, he has a positive, optimistic attitude. He believes that he will be able to apply what he has learned to any situation and acquire new knowledge when needed. _____

_____

_____

_____

2. Janet wants to pursue a career that will be satisfying, but she would also like to make as large an income as possible. She has decided to do what is fun and exciting now while she is young. She thinks there's a good chance that such work will lead to a high-paying position later. _____

_____

_____

_____

3. Gene has worked at several textile-related jobs during his college years, preparing for a career in textile research. He has taken advantage of his university's internship program and its summer job placement program. He is sure that with his education, experience, and contacts within the industry he will have no trouble finding a rewarding full-time position after graduation._____

_____

_____

_____

4. Claudia has a part-time job and a 2-year-old son. She is very interested in apparel technology but cannot attend classes. Instead, she is taking courses electronically from a nearby university. After paying course fees and buying the needed textbooks she logs onto computer sites for actual classroom lectures and demonstrations. She can "speak" to professors via e-mail. Then she takes the course exams for credit applied toward a degree. _____

_____

_____

_____

5. Clarise would like to have her own business someday. She is considering being a color consultant, having an evening gown rental shop, or owning a fashion boutique. Until she makes up her mind, she has decided to take business and marketing courses at the local community college. _____

_____

_____

_____

(Continued)

6. Diedre has a natural flare for fashion but has never applied herself to her schoolwork. She has decided that she can be a big success in the fashion world without spending the time and effort on advanced education. She plans to go after good jobs by telling employers she has whatever qualifications and experience they are seeking. She will use office politics to get personal credit for jobs done well and turn on her charm to get promotions. She plans to change companies often to hasten her climb up the career ladder.

_____

_____

_____

7. Fred is sure that he wants a career involving fashion. After high school, he is seeking training that will offer him a dynamic, professional, and useful education. He wants to have both a solid academic background and the practical skills needed to land a good job within the industry. _____

_____

_____

_____

8. Joel would like to be a retail buyer and eventually have a position in top retail management. Besides taking business and fashion courses after high school, he plans to include some technical apparel production courses. He knows that buyers often deal with contractors who manufacture private label goods for retailers. He wants to understand the process and be able to "speak their language." _____

_____

_____

_____

9. Regina started working in a retail store part-time during high school. She became a full-time employee after graduation. The store is pleased with her enthusiastic work. Regina realizes that she doesn't know everything and that she is gaining new knowledge each day. She learns from her mistakes and knows how to turn them into positive experiences. _____

_____

_____

_____

10. Louis has gained self-confidence through many extracurricular activities in school. Among other activities, he is president of the computer club and a member of the debate team. He feels that his computer skills and his ability to communicate a well-organized presentation will help him in the fashion firm where he hopes to work._____

_____

_____

_____

Employment Interests and Preparation

Activity D　　　　　　　　　　　　　　Name _____

Chapter 24　　　　　　　　　　　　　　Date _____ Period_____

Write answers to the questions under the headings *Employment Interests* and *Employment Preparation*. Then complete the evaluation questions.

Employment Interests

1. List hobbies, activities, and school subjects that you enjoy. _____
   _____
   _____

2. Would you prefer to work alone, with a few people, or with many people? _____
   _____

3. Would you prefer to work indoors, outdoors, or a little of each? _____
   _____

4. Would you prefer to work with ideas or objects? _____
   _____

5. Would you prefer heavy physical activity, light physical work, or desk work? _____
   _____

6. Do you prefer to work regular hours or have a varied schedule? _____
   _____

7. Do you prefer to lead a group or be a group member? _____
   _____

8. Rank the following "work values" in the order of their importance to you with 1 being most important and 8 being least important.

   _____ Achievement　　_____ Variety　　_____ Independence　　_____ Income

   _____ Self-expression　_____ Prestige　_____ Job security　　_____ Power

Employment Preparation

9. List tasks you do at home and describe how they prepare you for employment. _____
   _____
   _____
   _____
   _____

10. List school experiences that prepare you for employment. Include clubs or other groups in which you have learned leadership, communication, and other skills.
   _____
   _____
   _____
   _____

(Continued)

　　　　　　　　Chapter 24　A Career for You　199

11. Describe any part-time and summer jobs you have had as well as any volunteer work you have done.

_____

_____

_____

_____

_____

12. Check the following "good worker qualities" that describe you.

_____ Able to communicate effectively   _____ Enthusiastic

_____ Well groomed/suitably dressed   _____ Cooperative

_____ Tolerant of differences   _____ Cheerful

_____ Hard worker   _____ Honest

_____ Able to take orders/follow directions   _____ Punctual

_____ Accurate worker, even under pressure   _____ Self-confident

_____ Respectful/considerate of others   _____ Adaptable

_____ Dependable/reliable   _____ Courteous

_____ Able to take and handle criticism   _____ Well-organized

Evaluation

13. Which fashion careers are suited to your interests and preparation? _____

_____

_____

14. What specific additional preparation might you need to enter the field that interests you most?_____

_____

_____

15. Where or how can you get the additional preparation? _____

_____

_____

16. Reviewing what you have written, what course of action might you take concerning your future career?

_____

_____

_____

_____

_____

_____

_____

_____

_____

_____

_____

Applying for Employment

Name _____

Date _____ Period_____

Complete the following application for employment.

THE Southwest CENTER   DEPARTMENT STORE DIVISION

APPLICATION FOR EMPLOYMENT

NAME (LAST — FIRST — MIDDLE)		SOCIAL SECURITY NO.	DATE

PLEASE MENTION ANY OTHER NAME UNDER WHICH YOU HAVE WORKED OR BEEN EDUCATED

PRESENT ADDRESS (NO. AND STREET)	(CITY OR TOWN)	(STATE)	(ZIP)	PHONE NUMBER

WHAT HAS PROMPTED YOUR APPLICATION TO OUR COMPANY?

POSITIONS DESIRED:	MINIMUM SALARY REQUIRED
1.	
	DATE AVAILABLE FOR WORK
2.	

	YES	NO		
HAVE YOU EVER PREVIOUSLY APPLIED FOR EMPLOYMENT WITH THIS COMPANY?			WHERE	WHEN
HAVE YOU EVER BEEN PREVIOUSLY EMPLOYED BY THIS COMPANY (INCLUDING THE GLOVER DIVISION)?			WHERE	WHEN
IF YOU ARE NOT A CITIZEN OF THE UNITED STATES, DOES YOUR VISA OR IMMIGRATION STATUS PREVENT LAWFUL EMPLOYMENT?				
DO YOU HAVE ANY PHYSICAL DEFECTS OR CHRONIC AILMENTS THAT WOULD LIMIT YOUR PERFORMANCE IN THE POSITIONS STATED ABOVE?			DESCRIBE	
HAVE YOU EVER BEEN CONVICTED OF SHOPLIFTING, THEFT, OR OTHER FELONIES?			DESCRIBE	

EDUCATION

NAME AND ADDRESS OF SCHOOL	DATES ATTENDED		MAJOR STUDY	DEGREE RECEIVED	GRADE AVERAGE
	FROM	TO			
HIGH SCHOOL ADDRESS					
COLLEGE OR UNIVERSITY ADDRESS					
BUSINESS OR TECHNICAL ADDRESS					
OTHER ADDRESS					

HOBBIES, SPORTS, SCHOOL AND OTHER ACTIVITIES WHICH MAY HAVE CONTRIBUTED TO YOUR JOB SKILLS	TECHNICAL OR BUSINESS SKILLS INCLUDING SPECIAL COURSES AND TRAINING
_____	_____
_____	_____

MILITARY SERVICE

IF YOU HAVE SERVED IN THE U.S. ARMED SERVICES, WHAT BRANCH?

LENGTH OF TIME SPENT IN MILITARY SERVICE	HIGHEST RANK ACHIEVED

DESCRIBE DUTIES AND TRAINING _____
_____

PLEASE COMPLETE OTHER SIDE OF APPLICATION

(Continued)

EMPLOYMENT RECORD

START WITH PRESENT OR
MOST RECENT EMPLOYER   PLEASE LIST EVERY EMPLOYER INCLUDING PART TIME

NAME OF COMPANY		FROM
ADDRESS		TO
TITLE OR POSITION	NAME AND TITLE OF IMMEDIATE SUPERVISOR	
DUTIES		
REASON FOR TERMINATION		SALARY

NAME OF COMPANY		FROM
ADDRESS		TO
TITLE OR POSITION	NAME AND TITLE OF IMMEDIATE SUPERVISOR	
DUTIES		
REASON FOR TERMINATION		SALARY

NAME OF COMPANY		FROM
ADDRESS		TO
TITLE OR POSITION	NAME AND TITLE OF IMMEDIATE SUPERVISOR	
DUTIES		
REASON FOR TERMINATION		SALARY

NAME OF COMPANY		FROM
ADDRESS		TO
TITLE OR POSITION	NAME AND TITLE OF IMMEDIATE SUPERVISOR	
DUTIES		
REASON FOR TERMINATION		SALARY

REFERENCES

PLEASE DO NOT INCLUDE FRIENDS OR RELATIVES. LIST THE NAMES OF THREE PERSONS FAMILIAR WITH YOUR CHARACTER, ABILITY OR EDUCATION FOR MORE THAN ONE YEAR.

NAME	POSITION	COMPANY OR INSTITUTION	ADDRESS

PERMISSION IS GRANTED THE S.W. CENTER TO INVESTIGATE MY PERSONAL HISTORY AND SOLICIT STATEMENTS FROM ANY PERSON OR ORGANIZATION WITH WHICH I HAVE EVER BEEN ASSOCIATED. IN CONSIDERATION OF THE RECEIPT OF THIS APPLICATION BY THE S.W. CENTER, I RELEASE SAID COMPANY AND ALL PERSONS OR ORGANIZATIONS FROM ANY LIABILITY ARISING FROM SUCH STATEMENTS, THEIR SOLICITATION OR USE.

FAILURE TO PROVIDE COMPLETE AND ACCURATE INFORMATION ON THIS APPLICATION WILL CONSTITUTE GROUNDS FOR IMMEDIATE DISMISSAL. I ALSO UNDER-STAND THAT I MUST PRESENT PROOF OF DATE OF BIRTH WITHIN 30 DAYS FOLLOWING EMPLOYMENT.

I AGREE THAT IF I AM EMPLOYED I WILL ACCEPT THE TERMS OF BENEFIT PLANS FOR WHICH I BECOME ELIGIBLE AND THAT I WILL FOLLOW THE RULES AND POLICY PROVISIONS DESCRIBED IN THE EMPLOYEE HANDBOOK.

_____
SIGNATURE OF APPLICANT

IT IS THE POLICY OF THE S.W. CENTER TO PROVIDE EQUAL EMPLOYMENT OPPORTUNITY TO ALL APPLICANTS AND EMPLOYEES WITHOUT REGARD TO THEIR RACE, COLOR, RELIGION, SEX, AGE, NATIONAL ORIGIN OR HANDICAPS.

F603-8 (7/86)